# ROUGHNECK DADDY

*: A Memoir*

## Donna F. Orchard

ISBN: 0615407773
ISBN-13: 9780615407777
Library of Congress Control Number: TXu1-647-628
Donna\Forchard

for Al and Benjamin

for Clara, Wells, Ella, and Mack

In ways I don't fully understand, this story is connected to the lives and deaths of the following: James Taylor Fulmer, Marion Denterlein Fulmer, Gary Keaton, Clara and Gorman Keaton

# ACKNOWLEDGEMENTS

I want to thank Jim Fulmer and Marilyn Sewell who gave me the freedom to tell their stories too.

I owe an extraordinary debt of gratitude to my sister who introduced me to the loveliness of words: stories, poetry, essays.

A special thanks to my editor, May Laughton, for her steady direction, and idea to do a second printing. Many thanks to Frances Caldwell for her generosity and practical wisdom from early on. Thank you, Tom Larson, *The Memoir and the Memoirist,* whose workshop set me on this path. To Cynthia Rush for her editing help. And to Fred Marchman, my wonderful artist friend, for your help on the cover and anything else I asked you to do.

I'm grateful to all my school children over the years who made teaching such fun.

And much love to my Al-Anon friends whose vision for me keeps me going year after year.

A big 'thank you' to the Fairhope Public Library that provided a beautiful and quiet place to work.

## Donna F. Orchard

It is impossible to adequately express my appreciation to Bill Orchard, my partner in this effort, who makes my writing life possible. His tireless intelligence challenges me more than I sometimes want. He has answered my questions and been unreserved in his encouragement of my work.

Based on a True Story

This is an expanded version of an earlier work of the same title published in 2010.

**rough.neck**\ n (1836) **1 a**: a rough or uncouth person **b**: ROWDY, TOUGH **2**: worker of an oil-well-drilling crew other than the driller

# - 1 -

# THE SNATCHING

Cincinnati, Ohio
1950

I didn't know it would be tonight.

Daddy's big hands sweep me up out of bed and tuck me into the back seat of an old black car between my brother and sister. I crawl over Jimmy so I can see, but the moon and all the stars, erased. Only black. Soon the tires are between railroad tracks that rattle us from side to side, until we come to a steep hill and start up high, high, even higher on a bridge over dark green water.

I can't see. Where am I going? This was my first memory.

I try not to look over, but I can tell we're right on the edge. The car shakes and the tires squeak. Daddy can swim so he could save me but that's a long way down.

"I'm afraid of bridges. Do we have to go up?"

"Shut up, Donna," Jimmy says. "This is the way to Louisiana, stupid!"

Marilyn looks up from her book. "Hush, she's only three-years-old," shining a flashlight into our faces. She usually doesn't hear anything when she's reading. And I've never heard her take up for me.

Daddy turns around, "You kids settle down. Your granddaddy's trying to drive his Studebaker between the tracks on this bridge. It's narrow. You'll make him nervous."

I pull back on the half-open window so we don't fall off the side, the first time I use my special powers, peeking through my fingers when we get to the top. I jump back onto Jimmy and freeze when I can see straight down—down, down, down—miles into the black water.

I hear a big splash. Eyes move around down below. I think I see eyes.

"Get off me," Jimmy pokes my stomach.

"Where's Mama?"

"Oh, my gosh," Jimmy says. "Don't you know anything, Donna?"

"I'm not dumb. You're dumb!"

"Now be quiet, Donna," Daddy reaches back and pats my legs. "Put your head down, baby, and go to sleep. We'll be there by the time you wake up."

I'll probably die before then. I'm going to stay awake so I won't be surprised when it happens. If I'm gonna get eaten by an alligator, I sure don't want him sneaking up on me.

Everybody falls asleep while Big Papa is driving, except me; I keep one eye open to keep us safe.

I know she's not coming. At the end of every fight with Mama, Daddy shook his head and said, "I'll have to take these children to Loos'ana where I'll have help with them. I've got to work ..."

He didn't have to tell me straight out that Mama was too sick to take care of us. Some days she'd tell the nuns she had an emergency and drop me off at school with Jimmy and Marilyn. *I'm not supposed to be here.* Sister Mary Joyce sat me down in a big desk in the back of the room, the funnies out of the newspaper flopped down on the top to keep me quiet, my dangling feet in the air. *I'm too little to go to school.*

Finally, the bell rang at the end of the day and Mother was still not there to walk us home, so Marilyn took us to the play yard in the back of the school.

"I'm thirsty. Where's Mama?" Jimmy and I begin to complain.

"She had an emergency, Donna, Just be quiet. She probably just forgot what time it was."

As the hours wore on, it became just a dusty place to wait—not playing. Just waiting.

"There she is turning the corner!" I yell.

Mother ran up out of breathe, laughing and hugging us without explanation; everything forgiven, we walked home asking what's for dinner. She was too nervous to have us inside while she cooked.

At night when Daddy came in from his work in the candy department at Krogers, I ran to put my hand in his deep side pockets, sure to be stuffed with Fireballs, Tootsie Rolls and Jawbreakers.

"Why are your shoulders so red, Donna?" Daddy asked me. Then they'd start to argue. "Marion, I thought I told you not to leave these children alone like that. For God's sake, Jimmy fell off the slide last fall and had to have stitches. They called me at work when they couldn't find you. You don't have to work. All you've got to do is take care of these children. I pay the rent on this damn house. I want them home when school is out!"

"Jim, calm down. The cross-city bus wasn't running today, so I had to take the next one. I took Mother to the doctor and ..."

"Your mama. It's always your mama. She's out on her front porch drunk every day, eating Limburger cheese and drinking raw eggs. It's disgusting. And there you are right beside her. These are your kids! Don't you understand I can't work always worrying about these children?"


Jimmy remembers, "Geez, I forgot all my toys!"

I sit up and grab the flashlight from Marilyn to look around the car. I told Daddy to look up high and reach the bride doll. Marilyn says it's hers, but it's mine. I told Daddy to get it. Where is it?

I think Mama was up the hill spending the night with Grandma Kay again when we left. She's going to be mad when she sees the bride doll missing from that cabinet. Mama doesn't let us play with it much because of her long white dress and veil.

I wonder what my puppy's doing. Daddy told me, "Big Papa won't let you put that dog in his car." He promised to get me another puppy when we get to Granny's house.

## Roughneck Daddy: A Memoir

I bet my puppy's looking for me right now. I tap Daddy on the shoulder in the front seat, "Are we almost to Granny's house? Can I get another puppy tomorrow?"

Daddy wakes up, "Do I hear you crying, baby?"

"I'm thinking about my puppy, Daddy. Who we going to see in Louisiana?"

"Your Granny Fulmer will be glad to see you when we get there. You were born in Loos'ana but we moved back to Cincinnati when you were just a baby."

"How long are we going to stay there? What does she have to eat?"

Big Papa points to a sack, "Here, baby, your granny sent some cold cut sandwiches for us. James, give that baby something to eat."

"Come on up here in the front seat and sit in my lap, Don." That's what Daddy calls me, just half of Donna.

"I'm glad you woke up, Daddy. I'm scared."

"Scared of what, baby?"

"Alligators."

"What alligators?"

"The ones down under the bridge."

"Alligators don't live up here in these waters, honey. Alligators live in swamps down South, where we're going. But Daddy won't let any alligator eat up his baby."

Out of nowhere, I think about my Sunday shoes, in the shoe box under the bed. "Did you get my Sunday shoes, Daddy, my black patent leather shoes under the bed? Oh gosh, I forgot to look under there. They weren't thrown in the sheet with my panties and socks when I emptied my drawers, were they?"

"I can't remember where everything is, Don. We'll find them when we get there."

Jimmy looks around at Daddy, "That sheet stuffed with clothes looked like a giant parachute when you tied it at the top and threw it over your shoulder."

"Will you swing me in that sheet like a bucket when we get there? We haven't done that in a long time ..."

"Sure. Calm down now, Don. Daddy's here. Go on back to sleep."

I hear my Big Papa's voice, "James, did you give the children some sandwiches? We don't have time to stop for food. I told the sheriff to meet me at the parish line with the papers after the judge signs them. Won't be anybody taking these Fulmer children back."

When the car finally stops under the sign, 'Fulmer Street' Jimmy punches Marilyn,

"We're going to live on a street named after me!"

Big Papa stands up and I look at him for the first time since he drove all the way. He's extra tall and has a nose bigger than Daddy's. Still in a suit and tie he asks me to reach back in the car for his red can of tobacco and starts to stuff his pipe. "You are home now, children."

My grandmother swings the front door open and hugs me first when we arrive after our long trip from Cincinnati. "Come here, baby, I'm your grandmother. Do you remember me?"

"Yeah." But I really didn't.

"Yes Ma'am, Donna." Granny cuts me off quick.

"Oh, Yes Ma'am."

Granny is all round and soft. She's a lady, with ruffles around the neck of her house dress and curls in her silver hair. She walks slower than my mama.

"Come on inside and have something to eat. Those men didn't let you children stop for snacks did they? Well, you're here with Granny now and I always have tea cakes in that big yellow cookie jar. You can go in there anytime you want to."

As I step inside the house, "It smells funny in here."

"Be quiet, Donna," Marilyn catches my arm.

We stand in the dusty living room, and I look over at the fireplace with windows all around. Big Papa puffs out his chest, proud of his house. We open the double doors into the dining room and Granny says that will be my bedroom, and Marilyn's. "Where will we sleep?"

"Hush." Marilyn gives me the look again, her black eyebrows raised, "Go sit on the window seat."

"The white window seat runs clear across the back of the room. "Hey, the part you sit on opens up. Look at all this junk in here: a red plastic flower pot that's cracked, Santa Claus paper, oh here's a yo-yo." Throwing the yo-yo behind me, the string whirls around Marilyn's leg. "Oh, Donna."

I fall on the floor laughing as she tries to get the string off. "Sorry."

I look out the window and can't wait to go exploring when it gets to be morning. I want to see Granny's flowers she brags about and the big oak tree that's a hundred years old. I jump when I hear somebody walking in the yard. I'm scared, but I see it's Daddy, who goes under the street light holding a brown bag. He was just inside with us.

I continue plundering under the window seat and decide nobody would come wanting to use any of this stuff.

Later I wake up stretched out on top of the seat with Granny rubbing my back. "Come on in here, baby, and get in my bed. You can sleep with me until your bed is put up and Marilyn can sleep on the day bed beside us. I know all you children are tired."

The next day Daddy moves the fancy dark dining table over enough to put up our bed, but nothing else changes much. Granny's silver knives and forks are hidden in a brown box in a long, high table along one wall. On the other wall is a showy glass cabinet with blue flowery plates and fancy glasses that jingle when I walk on the wood floor. Daddy puts a wire hanger over the door for our clothes, but our winter coats won't fit.

"Where can I put my panties and socks, Marilyn?"

"Look in that chest down under the china. There's a drawer there," Marilyn tosses her winter clothes on the bed.

"Wow, look at the fancy pajamas. The whole drawer is full of these silky things, pink and blue with lace."

"Close that, Donna, and don't go in there again. I forgot. Granny pulled out that drawer and told me that's where she keeps her special gowns, the ones she's saving for when she goes to the hospital."

"When is she going to the hospital?"

"I don't know. Gee. Get back to work."

"Hey, what about that long window seat? It opens."

"Let's look. It's full. Tell you what, Donna; we'll stack the stuff we can fold on the dining table. You're here and I'll be over there. I get more room because my clothes are bigger."

When I finally get away from Marilyn and her trick questions—the ones she's going to answer herself—I find Jimmy in a rocking chair on the front porch. He's chewing on a stalk of sugarcane to get the sweet out.

"Let's go down the hill. I saw some boys playing baseball." I pull on his leg.

Jimmy slaps his knee, "Man, I don't have my glove!"

"Donna, go ask Granny if we can go play with some of our new neighbors."

"Donna can go with you, but look out for her, Jimmy," Granny means it.

"I know," he yells as he grabs a tea cake.

That night, I wash my long blond hair that becomes a mess of tangles. "I hate my hair!" I take a comb and yank the rats out until I'm standing there with hunks of hair in my hand. I yell and scream until Granny motions to me, "Come sit down here beside me." She divides each strand with her crooked fingers and combs and combs and combs and talks to me.

"Remember you're a little girl, Donna. You've got to grow up and become a young lady."

That's going to be a long- drawn- out job for my old granny, since being a girl is something I hope the boys forget when I find loose balls for them. I'll be glad when I'm big enough to be chosen for a team.

We settle into our life in Homer with Granny, Big Papa and Daddy. My new neighborhood's all boys, except for Marilyn, and she doesn't count. She stays inside most of the time making rosettes or reading a thick book and can't throw a baseball very far anyway.

The backyard down the steep steps becomes my favorite place to play when I'm home alone. The back is for gathering eggs, feeding the rabbits, picking green apples, gathering figs before the birds peck them apart or shooting some hoops on the dusty basketball court. A couple of times a year, Big Papa shows up with one of Mr. Blanton's horses to plow the garden to plant tomatoes, musk melons, beans, peas, and squash.

Unless it's killing day. On that day my gentle grandmother turns into a butcher to fill the freezer with hens and fryers.

Some of the chickens are my pets—dyed bitties colored blue, green, and pink I get for Easter. They have names, but I don't know which ones are mine after the colors wear off.

When the water starts boiling over the wood fire, Granny goes out to the hen house to catch a squawking chicken. After she runs one down, (with her apron blowing up over her face), she sits by the fig tree and throws its neck 'round and 'round while that chicken flaps and claws and yells, blood flying everywhere. When it gets good and still, she hangs the dead chicken on the clothes line, then one at a time sticks them in boiling water so the feathers are soft and easy to pull out. Scalding chicken feathers is a smell you never forget.

"Donna, get your old clothes on and come help me pluck these chickens."

"Are you through with the killing?"

"Yes, baby. I'll put the step stool here so you can reach the clothes line. Now grab me one of those fryers."

I view my granny different after that first killing in the backyard, but we're close. After the work is done, I'm ready to take a nap and so is she. The attic fan blows strong through the row of tall windows by the bed, all hot air, but I get sleepy. Granny's arms are soft and floppy and I nudge up to her as close as I can get, both of us sweating, and I beg to hear one of the old stories until my eyes close.

I learn fast to crawl up on the kitchen cabinet for cereal, to steal hand-me-downs out of my sister's drawer, and to never ask for Mama. Nobody mentions her, even in secret, except when Daddy gets drunk. Somebody decides that's the best way.

Daddy goes back to his job as a roughneck, sometimes gone for days at a time. I know it's rough work because Daddy and all his friends have big calluses on both hands. He doesn't tell me much about the rig when he laces up his steel-toed boots, puts on his tin hard hat, grabs his lunch, and kisses me good-bye. He shakes his head and says, "An oil well is a different world, baby, a different world."

I lie in bed knowing he's up in the derrick and wonder what I'll do if he takes a step the wrong way and

**Donna F. Orchard**

falls, suddenly leaving me alone with my grandparents, clearly so old they might croak at any minute.

Then what will I do for cereal?

# - 2 -

# THE FIFTEEN YEAR VISIT

Homer, Louisiana

This is where this part of the story begins since I never saw the face of my great grandfather, James Joseph Fulmer, who's buried somewhere around Etoil, Texas; except for one picture where he's lined up with members of the Masonic Lodge, upright dignified men in aprons, embroidered cowls down to their waists. And that's not a picture to be passed around to average folks or women. I expect that at my great grandfather's wake, a Mason sneaked the picture out from under his coat and gave it to my Big Papa who wears the black ring too.

My grandfather had a big bunch of brothers and two sisters. Well, you might as well say one sister. My great-aunt Edna got tuberculosis when she was a girl and they sent her to Boonville, Arkansas, to a sanatorium for twelve-year quarantine. When it was time to get out, she'd been there most of her life and decided to stay.

Big Papa's wild brother, Bill, got the Fulmers from Texas to Louisiana. They had to hotfoot it out after Bill went and killed a man during an argument. Leroy, Eb, and Bill ran to North Louisiana hoping the law would give out before they did. That dead body changed just about everything for the Fulmers.

Recently, at a family reunion, my brother and I were talking about our great-uncle Bill. "Donna, do you think he was saved?"

"Well, I know he was saved one day from the law when he made it to Louisiana where he married five times, a younger woman each time."

Jim, my daddy, was a roughneck and the black sheep of this present set of kin and picked up where his wild Uncle Bill left off.

JAMES JOSEPH FULMER (FAR RIGHT ON END)

Daddy doesn't fall out of the derrick, but when I'm seven years old he does show up at the hospital with half a forefinger. You can see it in all his pictures after that, because he always poses with his hands on his hips.

Big Papa gets a call from Dr. Pat to say Daddy's had an accident on the rig—his finger. They found it in his glove. They've already sewed it back on. We rush to the hospital and see his big fat pointer all wrapped up. He's not in bed, but pacing up and down the hall cussing that finger with every step he takes. After a few days when he's still walking in pain, he tells the doctor to "cut the damn thing off. I don't need it."

Daddies don't know when girls need panties and slips but they do know that little girls need a new pair of shoes ever so often. When Daddy picks up my old shoe, looks through the hole, and sees daylight all the way to the floor, we plan our shopping trip for the next time he's off.

We go to White's Dry Goods on the town square. It's a circle around the big white courthouse with huge pillars that reach into the clouds, a statue of a young Confederate soldier out front. He looks about fifteen years old. The saddest face I've ever seen. Marilyn says the people in Homer never surrendered. I don't know what she means. Anyway, you have to drive around that circle to get anywhere, so I don't know why it's called the town square.

"Hi Miss Altaline. Fix Donna here up with some shoes," Daddy talks to her familiar, like he's talking to family. "This child is rough on her shoes. I don't have to bring Marilyn up here but a couple of times a year."

After I walk out wearing the new white Mary Janes, if Daddy's feeling good, we go to the Purple Cow Café and have a "Burger Basket," a burger hidden under mounds of onion rings. His buddies are already there: Junior Palmer with wide nostrils, and his son, Dub, big Randall Childress, and Buddy Emerson—all roughnecks, drinking and fighting buddies.

"Good to see you, Jim. I heard about your finger," Junior says. "Isn't like you to have no accident."

"Aw, I was clamping the tongs on the casing when I put this finger in a hole and the damn pipe shifted. Got the top of it down to the second knuckle," he held up his bandaged finger." I've come mighty close, but that's the only time I ever got hurt on a rig in all these years."

Daddy and his friends talk in front of me. They let me listen to their stories that always end up with one of them "knocking somebody on their ass." No matter how rough the talk gets, I don't act surprised. Daddy never mentions the café to Granny when he shows her the shoes.

It's not like Daddy and his buddies set out to fight, but after a whole night of poker, washing down every losing hand and all the others with "White Lightning" bootleg hooch, it usually turns out that way.

One Saturday night, Daddy lets me go with him if I promise to sit in the corner and stay quiet. They sit down for a poker game at the garage across from the cemetery. Daddy wins a big pot because I'm good luck for him.

Junior who hates to lose goes over to Daddy, "You cheated me, you son-of-a bitch."

"Are you calling me a cheater, you bastard?" Daddy turns red. "I'll tear your head ..."

"Come on. Try it. Get up you son-of-a bitch. Get up and show me what you got."

Shorty jumps up, "Okay, boys," he rolls his eyes, "Here we go again. Sit down! I need to win my money back."

I'm afraid of Junior Palmer. He's always talking 'some shit,' Daddy says, trying to get back at somebody for something.

He and Daddy calm down and go back to the poker game that night but the fight isn't over.

They both ride around in broad daylight with a rifle in the back window to let the other one know, this threat is for real. Daddy goes for weeks yelling, and cussing, and threatening Junior when he calls.

I start to shake and run to the door when I see a car pull up with "Sheriff" on the side. This is the first time the police have ever come to our house. Mamie, our neighbor, is already standing out in her front yard being nosey. I know what it's about.

The sheriff has a big star on his chest, a cowboy hat to match the brown shirt and cowboy boots; all I can see are the pointy toes.

"Jim, now you and Junior settle down. And take that damn rifle out of your back window, you hear, before you and your boys get into some serious trouble." He won't move until Daddy goes over and gets the gun out of the car. He walks to his car slowly, looking back over his shoulder to let Daddy know he means what he says. Big Papa is in the garden and I keep my fingers crossed he doesn't see a sheriff at his house. That would be real trouble.

Daddy never shoots Junior, but somebody does.

The phone rings late one Saturday night so the first thing I do is run to see if Daddy's home. Then I hear him talking to somebody. He hangs up and his face turns pale. Junior got shot at the gas station on the White Lightning Road. Daddy says I can go with him to see how bad Junior is hurt.

When we get out in the parking lot, Daddy catches my arm for me to stop. A white chalk line outlines a body on the cement where Junior fell. I figure he's dead.

What would make somebody so mad that they decide not just to threaten Junior, but to really shoot him?

Do they draw a line around everybody when they die?


I catch on from Daddy and his buddies what's little and what's big in adult talk.

One day, in the next room, Daddy begins telling Granny about a conversation he has with Hazel Key who lives right around the corner, my second cousin once removed. Seems that right in the middle of their talk about Tom's arm getting numb and tingling all the way to his neck, Hazel asks Daddy, "Can I have Donna?"

I stay quiet as a stowaway behind the couch. Is Daddy going to make me go over to Hazel's to pick up pecans for her again? As I hold my breath, I begin to realize, it's more serious than that. I hear Daddy say to Granny, "Hazel asked me if she can take Donna, to raise, since she can't have children of her own." Daddy has three so I guess she figures she'll take one off his hands.

At seven years old I get a big lump in my throat and start to cry since I already know that Tom Key is a worse drunk than Daddy because I saw him back his car all the way around the corner, and up the hill to our house saying, "I get tired of driving forward." And Hazel Key smells like Ponds Cold Cream, and her house too, and nobody much comes in and out the front door. Then Daddy says, "The nerve! I tell her quick I didn't go to all this trouble to keep my kids just to give one of them away. These children will grow up together."

That night I sit in Big Papa's lap to watch my favorite western while he puffs on his pipe, and blows perfect smoke rings. He teases me and gives me love pats on my bottom pretending to spank me.

I hope he'll forget to look at the clock. But he doesn't. At eight o'clock, he makes everybody, including Daddy, turn off the TV. The radio is turned on, and tuned in to *The Reverend. J. Hamilton Robbins in Del Rio, Texas.*

"Let me tell you about what you can do to help us in our ministry right here on the border with Mexico." the Reverend says through the round speaker at the top of the wooden stand up radio.

When the Rev. Robbins gets to the invitation he asks me to make a decision: "If you are taken tonight before tomorrow night's sermon on 102 .9 WPQS at eight o'clock; where will you go? Will you be greeted by your Maker?"

He goes on, "I've got something I want you to do between now and then. Tomorrow morning go stand in a cemetery close by where you live and look at those graves. Count them. Most of those people in that cemetery weren't willing to give up everything. They told the Good Lord, 'No.' Ladies and Gentlemen, be careful about telling the Good Lord, 'No.' He will ask something of you; will ask a lot of you. What will He change in your life and mine? Everything. He may even ask you to go to Africa, to win the souls of the heathen. Will you go?"

We don't have orange juice, but Africa's probably worse. I may get somebody harder to share a room with than Marilyn. I'm not going.

"Next, do this for me. Go to the top floor of a building. Get on the elevator and press 'down' and go as far down as you can go. Imagine you are descending into a fiery hell. How does that feel?

Then press 'up' and go all the way up, all the way to the top on that elevator. Imagine that you are going into the gates of heaven, greeted by Saint Peter. Now, my friends, which way will you go?"

By this time I'm trembling. I know I'm a bad little girl. My library book has been sitting on the window seat for two years. I lie awake and worry about it. I avoid even walking by the library. Why don't I just take the book back and pay what I'm sure will be hundreds of dollars in fines? I'm scared to ask Big Papa for the money and besides he doesn't have any money.

So during the singing of "Just as I Am," I study my decision, think of everything—streets of gold—everything; the preacher steady reminding me not to be a slacker, not to make a careless decision. Even if I did the worse thing in the world, like Jimmy did, when he put a hole in the colored window at the Methodist Church with his BB gun and never told anybody; even if I did something like that, I still wouldn't go to Africa. I choose hell.

I don't like to sleep by myself when Marilyn's gone, like tonight when she's staying with Miss Lera, the widow-woman across the street.

I don't mind praying. But when I get in Granny's bed after the sermon that night, good and sleepy, she carries on way past my limit.

Granny's praying starts with her seven children and goes to the others she raised as her own. Then moves to her grandchildren and great-grandchildren. "Bless Bernardine, Ernie, Varnell, Mellie, Gene, James and Lemos; then Sonny, Leroy, Lois Gwyn, and a special prayer for James. Lord, help him stop his drinking and to start going to church with these children, the last three I'll be raising." I figured it up one time that we're numbers eleven, twelve, and thirteen. She never mentions my mama.

When Granny quotes Psalm 103: *Bless the Lord, O my soul: and all that is within me, bless his holy name,* and ends with," Bless all to whom it is our duty to pray for, the world over, far and near," that's my signal to pray. Even though you'd have to agree, by this time, she's covered things with God from just about every angle.

When I'm about to fall asleep, I remember Daddy's still not home. I lie awake to make sure he makes it in from Ruth's, his girlfriend's house. I hope he doesn't get thrown in jail for going too slow. That's how Daddy drives when he's drunk.

Soon, I hear him pass my window. I know he tries not to wake his papa, but he bangs from one rail to the other on the steps before he makes it into the side door.

Daddy walks to the middle of the kitchen floor and pulls on the long light cord.

Did you know that roaches can fly? I listen to see if he puts a white bundle of butcher paper down on the counter and unwraps it—a big round steak enough for both of us. By the time he turns around to the ice box and takes a slug of buttermilk, I sneak out of Granny's bed and walk down the dark hall to peek in the kitchen. He acts surprised, "What ya doin' up, Don?" I know he wants me to cook that steak for him, just right—rare.

"You've been gone two weeks. Where you been? Granny and Papa were worried."

"I was down at the colored folks' camp, baby. I took some time off to stay with Essie Mae and fish; ate nothing but fish for two weeks. She's a sweet woman and she knows how to catch some fish, boy oh boy; big ones."

"For two weeks? She let you stay at her house for two weeks?"

"Go on, baby, and fry me that steak."

Daddy used to be a cook in a fancy restaurant in Washington, D.C., so he showed me how to cook his steak. You put it in the frying pan with a little garlic and turn the gas on as high as it will go. Count slowly to twenty, then flip it and count again. Spoon some juice on the top. Too rare for me. I turn off the gas and leave my piece in the pan. Granny says I take to cooking like Marilyn takes to sewing.

Marilyn doesn't want to be around Daddy when he's drunk, but I'll be with him anytime I can. Besides, this is the time for asking, when he's drunk and in a good mood.

"Mrs. Linton says I need glasses. I can't see the board. I told you six months ago. When can we go to Waskom to get me some glasses? I can't see. I'll make better grades if I can see, more A's like Marilyn."

"No you won't. You like to be outside all the time." He takes a bite of steak, "It's good, sugar—you'll be so rough on a pair of glasses, Don. They'll probably stay broken."

"Why can't we go to Dr. Woodman in Homer to get my glasses so we don't have to drive to Texas?"

"Woodman is crazy." What he really means is, 'I don't like the man. I think he'll charge me too much.'

"I told you I'd take you to Texas, baby doll, when Daddy gets a day off."

"Well, when will that be? In how many days?"

"You know I never know, Don. I told you I'd take you!"

"Okay."

The jitter-bug urge hits him and he slides off the brown vinyl dinette chair and across the floor. "Did I ever show you how I can dance, Don? Your mother and I loved to jitter-bug. You know, I'll never love another woman like I do your mother. I'll always love your ..."

"I know. Show me how you cross your hands over your knees again ... I can do it!"

He spins me around to make me giggle.

*I-I-I-I-I-I like mountain music*
*Good ole mountain music*
*Played by the real hillbilly band.*
*I like rural rhythm*
*That I might sway right with 'em*
*I think the melody is grand!*
*I hear Hawaiians play in the land of the wicky, wacky*
*I must say, I like "Chickens in the Straw" by crackie.*

Daddy stops dancing suddenly, gets real quiet, cups his hands, and starts crying, "Lord Jesus, I'm a dirty, rotten sinner. I beg you to forgive me this time and I'll never touch that stuff again. I know I don't deserve these three babies, these three good kids. Thank you for giving me these children. I'm going to straighten up and be the daddy I ..." By this time I slip off the chair and go back into bed. He's a good daddy. He drinks whiskey because he's nervous. I think God knows that.

He goes to the back room and flops in bed next to Jimmy.

The next morning he laces up his boots, grabs the brown paper bag, and gives me a quick kiss, "Bye, baby."

The time for asking, singing, and praying is over; over and forgotten.

I get my glasses in Texas about six months later.

JIM

# - 3 -

# THE HIGH BOARD

When the screen door opens I get a whiff of oil that gets stronger and stronger as it moves down the hall, a sweet smell because Daddy's home. It's been cold, so he has on two old flannel shirts with blue jeans and a yellow slicker suit under his arm. Daddy says the tool pusher, a company man, is the only one you'll ever see at the rig with his name on a 'Slumber J' patch. But his real name is 'Sonofabitch.'

"It was so damn cold last night, Don, nothing I lifted was light. It was hard for me to keep my head or my ass up. When I finally got a break to drink some hot coffee, I picked up my Thermos, unscrewed the top, and the damn thing popped! Busted all over everything when it hit the cold; broken glass all inside. I leaned back against the dog house and thought; this is a goddamn how do you do. Unlace these boots for me, will you, baby?"

Going straight for the tub. Daddy makes loud man noises, splashing, grunting and roaring, together with snorts, blowing and honking his nose. He kicks up a fuss with soapy water that sloshes up one side of the tub and down the other, soaking the whole floor.

He comes out of the bathroom with a clean shave. "Don, pare down these calluses for me before I put my socks on. My boots hurt me all night."

I take the straight-edged blade out of his razor and feel under his big toes. "Yeah, they need it." I can't go fast, trimming away the thick skin. I've never sliced him open, but I'm just eight years old, so he warns, "Now, be careful, baby, and don't cut me," just in case. Then after each bit of skin, he leans over and feels his foot until it's just right.

He's handsome in a white shirt, wet hair slicked down, perfumy with Aqua Velva cologne. I want him to stay at home awhile with me but he's steppin'out with his girlfriend, Ruth. A quick kiss, "Bye baby girl. I'll be back."

"When? When we going fishing again, Daddy?"

"We'll go the next time I'm off. I hear they're biting down from the spillway on Lake Bistineau."

In about two weeks, Daddy comes in around noon from a double shift and tells Jimmy and me to check the poles in the garage and to get them ready for fishing the next day. "Be sure each line has a sinker, cork, and a hook. Then go out back in the worm bed and dig us some big ones. We've got to get up about four in the morning. The bream'll be hitting early. Don, get Marilyn up when you get up."

I'm awake at three, and wake Daddy before four, excited.

"You know Marilyn's not going to get up," I complain to Daddy.

"I'll rouse her up. Watch me," Daddy sounds sure. "Sis, roll out. It's time to go. We're missing some big ones out there right now. You can snooze in the car."

"Why are you doing this?" Marilyn picks her head up when Daddy shakes her shoulder. "It's the middle of the night. I don't think I'll go this time."

"You're such a sissy," I chime in.

"I guess I'll go. Wake me up in fifteen minutes," Marilyn looks at me, "You little twerp."

I go out to the car with Jimmy and help him slide the poles in through the back window.

I know what everybody likes, so I make the sandwiches: hot mustard for Daddy. Mayonnaise and regular mustard for Jim and me, everything for Marilyn—does she have to have tomatoes and lettuce when we'll be in a boat? *I can't be doing all that.* I slap some ham on each one and stuff them in a bag.

"Fifteen minutes is up, I'm calling Jimmy to pull you out of bed," I let Marilyn know it's my last warning.

"No, no, Donna, get me my clothes, I'll get up. And make some breakfast for me, will you? And Donna, don't forget to butter my toast this time."

"Okay, if you'll get up when breakfast is done. Daddy's gone to buy some minnows."

The morning sun is hot even before the boat is rented at Lake Bistineau. The bait, fishing tackle, and lunch go under the middle seat.

We wade into the water, and are supposed to jump into the boat while Jimmy shoves it from the bank into the lake.

"I can't step up that high." I say looking at everybody else in the boat.

Daddy thinks he's so strong that he can hold a big eight-year-old like me. "I got you, Don," he says in his confident daddy voice.

When I get one foot in the boat, I start wobbling, "Let me go!"

"I got you, Don, just step over in here. I got you."

Suddenly I pull both of us off the boat and into the lake, fishing clothes and all. The two dry ones look at us and holler.

Daddy takes the soaking with surprising calm though, only a few dammits, sonsofabitches and chrissakes.

Jimmy pulls the boat back on the bank so I can get in. Daddy's in the front, drying out; I'm the middle, drying out; Marilyn's in the middle next to me pushing me away so she doesn't get wet; and Jimmy's in the back rowing.

Daddy warns me before we get to our fishing spot, "Now Don, don't move around and turn over the bait can. Remember what happened last trip? You have to sit down in a boat, baby."

"Okay, Daddy." I want to please my daddy more than anything, but I just can't stay still in a boat. People tell me I'm high-strung. I'm not sure what that means, but I know it's not good.

## Roughneck Daddy: A Memoir

I see that everybody else is catching bream, big bream, but me. And then I get a bite that pulls my cork way under the water. When I hop up to get a better hold, the boat tips up in the air, and BAM! There goes the bait bucket. All those minnows go belly up in the bottom of the boat. Daddy cusses, "I can't catch fish with dead minnows." I feel terrible and cry until I get another bite.

"That's the cypress tree right there, where a water moccasin slid out on a limb over the lake and fell into our boat last year. I think I see a snake up there right now."

"No you don't, Donna. Besides, he didn't fall in the boat last year. You were just afraid he might. Daddy knocked him down with the paddle. Gee, you make up things," Jimmy dismisses me.

"Well, he looked like he wanted to fall in the boat."

About the time we all get settled back down after rescuing a few minnow still alive, I felt something in my shoe. Something moved! There's a big hole in the bottom of one of my old fishing shoes. It may be a snake, it's slimmy! EEEK! I throw my shoe in the air. "Get it out! It's something black and wet. What is it? Get it out of my shoe!"

"It's just a leech, Donna," Daddy holds up the fat, black, slimy thing and chuckles with Jimmy and Marilyn.

I like to fish from the bank so I don't have to look at those dead minnows in the bottom of the boat and worry about leeches in my shoes. Jimmy comes up to compete with me when I start catching bream.

"Why doesn't Daddy ever take us with him to fish at the coloreds' camp?" I start meddling.

"He's not fishing, Donna. Why are you being so nosy?" Jimmy groaned. "Daddy goes there to get drunk. Big Papa won't let him drink at the house. Daddy keeps his whiskey in a paper sack out in the garage or under the seat of his car. When he gets off the rig after working twelve hour days, seven days a week for six months, Daddy goes on a bender."

"Huh?"

"When he shows up at Essie Mae's camp, she figures if he's determined to stay drunk for two weeks, she can at least see to it he doesn't die. She's a good woman and a friend."

"She lets him lie around her house drunk?"

"She can't stop him. He's gonna drink until the whiskey's gone. Then she watches him through the shakes until he starts to eat fish and can drive home."

"How do you know all about this, Jimmy?"

"Big Papa had to go get Daddy one time when Essie Mae thought he might die. I rode with papa out there."

We see Daddy fly fishing for bass before the day is over. "Jimmy, shhh! Stop rowing so they won't hear us." Daddy's hand is so big, he can paddle the boat over to the brush where the fish are. The fly line doubles back and sparkles in the sun as the lure falls to the perfect spot, near the brush growing along the bank.

## Roughneck Daddy: A Memoir

It's nightfall so we stop with plenty of bream and couple of nice bass. We scale 'em and gut 'em, salt and meal them down, right on the bank. The black iron pot goes right up on the flames and the fish and fries, with the skins on them, are thrown into the hot grease. Supper is all the fish and fries we can eat, catsup and a loaf of Wonder Bread.

It's a hindrance being a girl. I like my name 'Don' because guys know how to have fun. I wish I could go carousing like my daddy, the biggest carouser of all, or at least sleep in a tent all night like Jimmy.

"Why can't I go camping with Jimmy and Ronnie? I go bird hunting with them. Jimmy's leaving now. Please let me go." I'm building up to a tantrum.

"Donna, baby, you're a little girl. You don't know about these things just yet, but you can't go off with a bunch of boys overnight," Granny says, sounding kind even when she's telling me 'no,' which makes me madder.

"You are such an old fogy. I hate you!"

"Go sit on your red stool, Donna, and calm down. I'm your grandmother." She says *grandmother* in a holy way, like when she quotes scripture.

I get so mad I want to hit Granny with that black skillet I'm holding. I don't. Sometimes I scare myself when I throw a fit. I don't know when it's going to come busting out of me.

Still bored, I beg Daddy when he leaves for work to take me with him. "You let Jimmy go."

"There's nobody out on a rig but a bunch of men, Don. We lie around sleeping in the dog house and the men have to change their clothes in there. It's no place for a little girl."

"So." I know better than to yell at my daddy like I do at my Granny. Daddy's never spanked me, not once, but when he's mad, everybody stands still.

In June, when I'm ten years old Daddy comes in and calls for the three of us, "I'm going to Jena, down in South Loos' ana, for a couple of months on a job. Since it's summer, your Granny and I have decided that you children can go with me, on the job, if you want to. Jena's about four hours away so I can't jump in the car and come home every day or two to see about you."

"I want to go!" I answer first. It sounds like fun and I'll be with Daddy.

Jimmy wants to go too, but Marilyn's not so sure.

"Is there a watermelon patch near the rig where we can steal watermelons? Remember you said you break 'em open on the ground and eat all you want," I remind Daddy.

"I don't know about that. I'll have to work, baby. You never forget a thing I tell you, do you Don?"

Daddy gets us settled in an old, but clean, apartment house in Jena and tells Marilyn to keep an eye on Jimmy and me. "I'll check in on you kids when I can. There's food in the icebox."

I look in the cabinet, "Vienna sausage and sardines. That's daddy food. I'll make tacos with this hamburger meat tonight. Bingo, Little Debbie's chocolate cupcakes, with the white center and white squiggles on top. Granny never lets us have these, Jimmy. I told you it would be fun on our own."

"You mean boring, don't you?" Jimmy sounds sad. "I'm not so sure about this place. Where's the fishing? I brought my rod. Daddy's got to work every day. What's there to do?"

"You just miss Ronnie. I'll throw my stuff down and we can go out to the rig to watch Daddy." I tell him, trying to look on the bright side.

"I've been out on rigs lots of times," Jimmy says as he laces up his new red high tops.

"I haven't. Let's go."

We stand way back where Daddy tells us to.

He gets into the lift on the floor of the rig and rides to the top of the derrick. That looks like fun. Then he steps out on a little wooden plank, just a narrow piece of wood. That looks scary.

"What's he doing way up there, Jimmy?"

"He catches the pipe when it comes up. Then he leans out on that rope and hooks the pipe to go back down in the hole to drill deeper. Daddy brags that he doesn't wear a safety belt. Says he wants to be able to jump out of the way if a pipe swings his way.

"He's a good derrick man, not afraid of heights. You know how he's dives off the high board at the swimming pool?" Jimmy reminds me.

"Oh, I know what he calls 'swimming lessons'… He picked me up from the baby pool and threw me in the deep end to bob up and down while I called, 'Help! Help!' Then he turned his back to me and climbed to the top of the high board to do his swan dive for my friends. I made it to the side by the time he popped up out of the water after his drive."

"Well, it worked," Jimmy admits.

"I'm afraid of high places. I don't even like bridges. Look there's a rope all the way from the tip top of the derrick to the ground like a circus tent. Is that how he gets down, slides on that rope?"

"He'll ride back down on the elevator," Jimmy explains, "That rope's in case of fire or something."

"Why would things catch on fire?"

"I don't know. Stop asking me all those questions, Donna. Ask Daddy."

He comes in from the rig that night complaining, "They sent a damn worm up there to help me today, some college student off for the summer. That kid almost got me killed. I told him, 'Son, you get paid from the neck down.' I had to go to the dog house to cool off before I beat him to smithereens."

I look at his face, dark red from the heat, "I've never noticed those black spots all over your cheeks."

"That's oil that soaks into my skin, Don. I never look like I have a good shave."

When we get back to Homer, Daddy's on the night shift, so he takes us to school. When I wake him up after he's had only a couple hours of sleep, he yells from the bed, "Three and three." I put three eggs and three pieces of toast on the table for his breakfast and jump on him, "Rise and shine Daddy Lion." I made this up to get him in a good mood.

When he goes to the rig, I slip in Daddy's room to look at his magazines. They're lying on the floor by the bed, the ones he reads before he falls to sleep. I never see him buy them, but when I snoop, there's always a new one: *True Detective* or *Front Page Detective.* I peep inside: stories called "I Watched Him Love and Kill," and, "We Stole to Hold Our Men."

These stories remind me of all the bad things that can happen to change my life forever: Daddy decides to live at Ruth's, Daddy has a car crash, or Daddy and Big Papa have a knock-down-drag-out.

# Donna F. Orchard

JIMMY

# - 4 -

# ANGEL

I wake up to the smell of Sunday dinner cooking and hear Granny say, "Remember, James, Donna's going to be baptized today. I wish you'd go with us."

"Mama, you know I just came off the rig. I've got some business to take care of. Right now I need to get a bath," Daddy yells back on his way down the hall to the bathroom.

I perch on my red step stool beside the stove and watch Granny cook Sunday dinner—no recipes, just a handful of flour, a china cup of milk, a dash of baking powder, a pinch of salt,'oh, and an egg. We talk to the rhythm of her rolling pin on a floured board, until the dough is thin enough for the strips of light dumplings.

"That's okay, Granny. I knew Daddy wouldn't go to church. He says they're all hypocrites. What's a hypocrite?"

"Honey, I'm too busy to get into all that. Get in the tub after James is out."

"Daddy's going where he always goes. What we having? It smells good."

"Venison roast, fried chicken, these dumplings with the boney pieces, mashed potatoes and gravy. Think I'll make some biscuits and cornbread since it's Sunday."

"And banana pudding with the brown wavy top?"

"Sure. Hand me those ripe bananas. It's a special day."

Each piece of round banana is put in its place in the bowl, just so. I don't know why she can't just cut the thing up and throw it in. It all gets mushed up together anyway. I wait for each perfect layer of bananas and then put the cookies on before she adds the warm custard. "You forgot the vanilla in the custard, Granny!"

"Oh, honey, thanks. You're so smart. You're going to be a good cook."

Granny always wears her green stripped apron and I wear my small pink flowery one, both made out of feed sacks, the pretty ones made special for women to take after the feed is gone, to make dresses and blouses.

"How come you can do all this cookin' on Sunday when Big Papa says people shouldn't work? Says he can't rake the leaves."

"You ask too many questions, baby."

What Granny meant about "special day," is while I was at church the week before, I went down the aisle and took Brother Hall's hand at the end of the sermon. Whispering in my ear he said, "What would you like to tell me, Donna?"

"Well, I figure there might be a God and if there was one, I'm pretty sure it's not me."

That was good enough to get me baptized. I'm afraid I'd have to go to Africa if I'm too ready.

Granny was sick and missed church the day I went down that long aisle, but when I got home and told her, she said, "Now, Donna, you're special."

The next week, I try to be good: I take my library book back and kick Jimmy in the shins a lot less. I still don't like daddy's girlfriend, Ruth.

"I can't go up all those stairs to the baptistery, baby. Anyway, I want to sit with Papa and watch you." Granny sounds old.

"I can't go by myself, Granny. I'm a good swimmer, but I'm scared of this dunking face up in front of everybody. I know," I yell as I run out the back door, "Ida'll go with me. I'll get over there before she gets going to her church."

"Wait up, Donna. Let Ida Champ go on to her church today."

"No, Granny, she'll want to go see me get baptized. I told her last week when she came to do the ironing that I went down the aisle all by myself, and she said she's proud of me, that everything will be different for me now."

"Honey, Ida and her people have their own church. That just won't work. I know you love her, baby."

"You don't understand. Says she loves me like her own. You know me and Ida eat together in the kitchen. I want her to come with me. Please, Granny."

"Listen to what I tell you, Donna. You can't go over there by yourself anyway. We don't have much time. Go next door and see if Mamie can go with us and help you change."

"I have to take my clothes off?"

"No, honey, you can leave on your underwear. Brother Hall will give you a white robe to wear in the water."

"Is the water deep?"

"No deeper than shoulder-high."

"Will the water be blue like in the swimming pool or green like the lake? Is it cold?

What if he can't hold me? I'm ten years old. Daddy and Jimmy can't even pick me up anymore."

"He knows how to do it, baby."

"I'll drown if he drops me."

"He baptizes big adult men, Donna, now run on like I tell you."

The baptistery sits suspended in the air over the choir loft. I hope when my head goes all the way under, it doesn't throw a scare into me. A big splash might soak the blue haired ladies.

Mamie motions to me. "It's your turn, Donna. You look like an angel." Brother Hall reaches for my hand. I try to step forward in the deep, warm water. The water's not green or blue, but cloudy, and I can't see my feet anymore. I don't feel much like an angel when my robe starts to float around me like a fat balloon. Fear strikes me and I start to shiver, my legs shake. I can finally grab onto him.

They'll be surprised if I don't stand up and walk out of here. I imagine when my head doesn't come up; they'll know I've turned into a real angel. Everybody will be happy they were here today, to tell their friends, "I was there Sunday when God decided to take that little Fulmer girl right on home since she was already up so high."

"Donna Gwyn Fulmer, I baptize you in the name of the Father, Son, and Holy Spirit. Amen. You are raised to walk in a new life."

I get home and look around. Nothing's changed. Maybe this new part's not for me.

I go back to church after supper to stand up front and say my Bible verses. Granny makes me put on girl clothes, six starched cotton petticoats under my circle skirt that has watermelon slices all over the front.

"Donna Fulmer please step out and say the Beatitudes."

*"And seeing the multitudes, He went up into a mountain: and when He was set, His disciples came unto him:*

*And He opened His mouth, and taught them saying,*

*Blessed are the poor in spirit: for theirs is the kingdom of heaven*

*Blessed are they that mourn: for they shall be comforted.*

*Blessed are the meek: for they shall obtain ..."*

Oh, no, I see Brother Hall shaking his head. I must have got off on that one.

I start again.

*"Blessed are the meek: for they shall see God."*

I can see him mouthing the words:

*Blessed are the meek for they shall inherit the earth.*

Got it!

*"Blessed are they which do hunger and thirst after righteous-ness: for they shall be Filled."*

I'm back on track. That was an easy one.

*"Blessed are the merciful: for they shall obtain mercy.
Blessed are the pure in heart: for theirs… for theirs …"*
He's trying to correct me again. I'm getting out of here.

I run by the altar in tears, but I can hear Granny's voice plain and clear, "Donna, a Bible verse will come back to you in times of trouble."

DONNA

# - 5 -

# BAD MOONSHINE

I wake up to some racket like wood cracking. I open the door and see Daddy falling up the steps from one banister to the other as he tries to get into his bedroom.

I scream, "Big Papa, Big Papa. It's Daddy. He's real sick."

I have to shake him since he's even deaf in his good ear now.

"What's wrong, James?" Big Papa says with a jolt.

Daddy starts to roll over and over as he moans about some bad moonshine. "Please Papa, the pain. Call Dr. Pat. Get him quick. I'm dying. Get the damn doctor."

Big Papa sounds scared, "Dr. Pat you better get over here. It's James. He's in pretty bad shape."

"Here's a warm rag for your head," I try to make it better.

"Leave me alone, baby, I'm sick. I'm not gonna make it. Help me. Shit, goddamn. Somebody help me."

I turn around and Dr. Pat is standing in the door. He's the quietest man I know. Never uses extra words, only the ones he needs.

"How much did you drink, James? Can you hear me? Tell me what you drank."

Why is he asking him all those questions? My daddy's dying. He needs to hurry up and do something for him.

"Let me check your pulse."

Dr. Pat slowly opens his black bag and pulls out a long needle.

"This'll help you get some sleep tonight, James."

In a matter of minutes, he begins to gather up his needles and sharp, knife-like doctor belongings to put back in the bag. A regular person gets scared, can expect to cry or bleed, or die when he sees these tools. But I can tell Dr. Pat is just thinking about going back to bed.

He starts for the door, turns around like he forgets something, looks at us standing by the bed, then looks down at Daddy, "James, you're killing yourself."

The next morning, Daddy wakes up and hollers to me, "Three and three," as usual.

I know not to mention last night.


I wonder why Daddy has to work way up there in the derrick when his brothers wear suits and work inside. Uncle Gene is a county agent and Uncle Lemos is a college professor.

Big Papa likes to remind Daddy that he didn't get his schooling, quit school in the tenth grade. Papa made him go to work. "No son of mine's gonna sit around the house all day."

# Roughneck Daddy: A Memoir

Daddy became a roustabout on an oil rig. He painted, put tools up, and kept the place clean.

When he became a roughneck, he decided to work up in the derrick. "I don't want to be down on the floor with the worms. They'll get you hurt. Slumber J sends those college kids out on the rigs during the summer, and they don't know their ass from grass."

I lie awake when I hear the phone ring in the middle of the night because I know Daddy has to leave.

"Don, I work on the casing crew because of you kids. I don't have to follow the rig and be gone three or four months at a time."

"Why do they call you in the middle of the night, Daddy? What do you do when you get there?"

"Well, baby, they have to get the oil out of the ground quick. It's big money for Slumber J. When the driller is ready to find more oil, he calls in the casing crew. I go up in the derrick and attach more pipe so he can go deeper in the hole. It costs lots of money to drill a well. Sometime they use a diamond bit on the drill stem, if they have to go through granite."

"Diamonds?"

"Not like diamond rings Don, much bigger and not polished up. Did you know that the diamond is the hardest rock? It can cut through anything. Sometimes the bit falls off. That's when we have to sit around and wait."

"What do you do then?"

"Just play poker or sleep in the dog house. That's where we put our lunch, change clothes or rest on the bunks. If we wait for twelve hours and the driller's still not ready for us, we can go home."

"Do you get paid?"

"Damn right. Two dollars an hour wait time. We're short-handed right now. The young boys are working in the Gulf because they're paying more. It's something new, off-shore rigs. They're drilling to see if they can find oil under the water."

"Why don't you go?"

"Sometimes you need to be scared, Don. If we hit gas and there's a fire, I have to jump. I don't want to jump in no damn water. Just last week the rig next to ours caught on fire at night. They hit gas when one of the damn light bulbs around the derrick busted and the whole thing went up, lit up the sky. We could see it several miles away. The metal derrick just melted into a puddle down on the ground …, never seen anything like it. Everybody got out. The derrick man slid down the soft line."

I know Daddy's smart and could have gotten his schooling. His buddies tell me how he can figure out the height and depth of the pipe in his head before the driller can figure it up on paper. He brags about having 'horse sense.'

But Big Papa says Daddy won't take instruction. Aunt Mellie told me when Daddy was a boy and came to eat, many a time Big Papa would get mad at him, slap his head, and knock him back from the table.

Daddy is Granny's favorite.

## Roughneck Daddy: A Memoir

She loves to tell me the story about what Daddy did for Uncle Lemos, who's two years younger than my dad. "Lemos came home for a visit when he was finishing graduate school at Louisiana State University. He knew Lemos didn't have any money. Papa didn't have any money to give him; he had retired from the Post Office by then. Your daddy was working on a rig, making good money and bought himself a new pair of shoes. When Lemos walked out front to the car going back to school, James noticed Lemos's old worn out shoes. James took off his new shoes on the sidewalk and gave them to Lemos."

Granny brags about her special powers when it comes to my daddy. This surprises me because she gives Jesus credit for everything else. She says, "James went to Washington, D.C. to find work right before World War II because nobody was hiring roughnecks. He was gone months at a time. I'd sit back in my brown rocker and get him on my mind after my Bible reading. 'Well, James is on his way home,' I'd tell Papa. Then in a day or two he would call or show up at the door."

Granny doesn't know about my special powers with Daddy, that I can stare at the white line on the road and keep his tires from going into the other lane.

Each year in the summer, we have one day with Daddy all to ourselves. He curses Slumber J Oil Company for having a big picnic every year when what he needs is a raise, but we go. Ruth's never there.

Excited, I jump in beside Daddy in the new blue Ford, "Why don't you get some other color when you get to pick out a new car?"

"I like blue, Don."

Jimmy gets in. Marilyn's dumb not to go. Free food.

We turn in by Louisiana State Park and wind through the woods until we get to the dirt road. As we get closer, I see the smoke rising over the trees and know the ribs are already on the heavy iron grills only rough-necks can handle. When we're near the opening, I can smell those ribs. A little further up are Daddy's buddies standing around frosty tin tubs, free beer already iced down, overflowing, enough for the whole day.

"Daddy, these new shoes hurt my feet. I want to play."

"Just take 'em off and leave 'em in the car, Don."

"But what will I put on? This blister is bleeding already."

"Just go barefoot like you do at home, baby. Nobody will tease you."

"I'll beat you in horseshoes, Jimmy." I can never beat him batting, but if I'm lucky, I can beat him in horseshoes.

When we get to the bare spot to play, I pick up my four horseshoes. They're heavier than I remember. But it's not long before I start to get some sliders, leaners and even a ringer whirling around the iron stake.

"That's on accident," Jimmy says. He rolls his eyes as I hop around in a circle and do my wigwam dance and warrior yell. He still beats me. I try to keep an eye on Daddy to see how many times he's goes for the beer tub.

Did he forget what happened last year? He got into a cussin' fight and I cried. I told him I would never go anywhere with him ever again.

After Jimmy and I play horseshoes, Daddy walks by and sees me sitting on my dusty feet, crying.

He squats down and puts his arm around me, "What's wrong, baby?"

"People are looking at me. They think I'm too poor to have shoes."

"Oh, Don. You're such a pretty little girl, with a nice dress on. They know you have shoes. How about I bring you some strawberry shortcake?"

Since I forget my glove, I shag foul balls for the boys playing baseball for a couple of hours. When I go to the canteen for water, I hear Daddy's name.

"Jim, why the hell you jumpin' in my shit, you son-of-a-bitch."

"Wait a minute, Robert."

"You think I'm fucking scared of an old man?"

"You think I'm scared of some twenty-year-old worm? You punk. If they let you up in the derrick, you'd kill somebody. Don't put your hands on me."

"Please, Daddy," I run up, yank on his pants leg, and beg. "Remember last year? Jimmy and I are here. Please Daddy," I try to pull him toward the car, "Let's go. Let's go home. I want my granny."

"Let go of me, baby. Daddy's just having a little fun."

It's too late. The kid throws a punch right on his chin with a thud.

Daddy swings, staggers and misses. They start dancing around each other.

"Come on you bastard."

"I'll teach you to get into my fuckin' business."

Somebody yells, "There're gonna brawl."

A circle of sweaty men appear out of nowhere and push me out of the way, yelling at Daddy and the kid.

I jump up trying to see.

"Go. Go. Go."

"Knock the shit out of him, Jim—he aint even ripe."

I wouldn't fight anybody with fists as big as my daddy's.

"Come on, give me your money on Jim." The stack of bills gets so high the man has trouble holding them all.

"Who's gonna bet on the kid?" A man in the back by me has a stack of money on the kid. I see some men bet on both of them.

"Come on guys. Put money on your boy." I get pushed aside as men wave their bills.

Wiggling between two tall men, I peek through a tiny hole. All I see is Daddy's bare chest and fresh blood running out of his nose. I hear a smack. I pinch a man's leg to make him move over so I can see. Daddy's on the ground. The kid's bleeding from his forehead all down in his face and into his eyes. He begins to kick Daddy with his steel-toed boot. "That's not fair. Somebody stop it." Nobody hears me.

# Roughneck Daddy: A Memoir

The men are all happy there's a fight. Don't they know that's my Daddy? He could die.

I run to Jimmy. "Make him stop, Jimmy."

"You know I can't stop him, Donna. I'm going to play."

Men yell at Daddy from every direction, "Jim, Jim, Jim" and I can't see what's going on.

I run to the car and hide on the floorboard with my hands tight over my ears, "The Lord is my Shepard, the Lord is my Shepard, the Lord is my Shepard" until it gets quiet.

Daddy doesn't die. He staggers into the car all bloody to drive home. Jimmy falls asleep in the back seat. I grab the wheel when we go over the center line. Maybe this is the kind of trouble Granny talks about.

When we get home its suppertime. I look on the stove and decide I don't want greens and pot likker again. I use some excuse to run down to see Mamie and her husband, Mike. I don't have to knock, but just leap up through the door and holler for Mamie. She likes to pretend she's my mother—sometimes.

Mamie cooks the cornbread I like in one of those black pans that flips over, two pones at once, fluffier than Granny's. If I show up at the right time, they're sitting down to eat.

"You had supper, Donna?"

"No, Ma'am."

"Well, sit down right here and visit. Want something to eat? Is your granny sick?"

Mike pipes up, "Leave that baby alone, Mamie, and give her some supper." I get a smile and a wink. Then he pats me and whispers, "You're a little scrapper."

Mamie is the only person who talks to me about my mother. How tall and beautiful she is, how she lights up a room when she walks in, and how she throws her head back and laughs. "Here's a picture of you and your mother when you were about two years old. Every morning she'd bathe you, dress you up, and bring you down here for a visit. Your mother didn't drive so sometime we'd put you in the car and go to the grocery store. Your first words were, 'Mamie, bye, bye, car, car.' Marion was one of my best friends. I still miss her. I haven't seen her in years.

Marion, my mother, calls us at least once a month. Seems like it breaks in on something I'm fixing to do every time. Her voice is strange and doesn't sound like anybody else I know. Jimmy, Marilyn and I pass the phone around and make up excuses not to talk. She slurs, "I love you, doll baby."

"Yeah, I love you, too."

I do know she loves me because of all the phone calls and cards for every occasion: Christmas, birthday, Halloween, Easter, Valentine's Day. And she sends packages: little dry store-bought cookies, chocolate wafer candies with white beads on top, and frilly dresses I don't wear. One day I plan to meet her.

Most days in the summer, I put on my bathing suit, jump on my bike, and ride about a mile to the town swimming pool to cool off. One afternoon when I go down the hill by Mamie's house and turn the corner to go up the hill, a door in the trailer park opens. The driller's wife, who hasn't lived there long, sticks her head out, motions to me, and says in a sweet voice, "Donna, I have something for you." I wonder if she means me.

"I've been watching for you to come by." She holds up a green outfit. "This goes over your bathing suit."

The material sparkles with silver swirls from top to bottom.

"See, it ties in a bow around your neck."

I look down on the large front pocket, and on it is "Donna" stitched in silver ribbon.

I don't know what to say, so I jump on my bike, and start to peddle away. "Thank you," I call back to her. "I've never had anything with my name on it."

The "patch" is a field of red dirt next to the trailer park. After school, when it's time, kids come pouring out of their front doors with baseball gloves: Ronald, brothers Bobby and Billy, Perry, Jimmy, and me.

I play outside until Granny opens the back screen door and yells, "Yahoo, Donna."

Always the same reply, "I can't miss my last bat."

Our house is dark even in daylight. I hate to go inside. Granny and Big Papa are either sick or talk about their friends who are sick, or think they're dying or talk about their friends who are dying, or if the friends are already dead, Granny gets on the party line to give every detail of the wake and who brought store-bought cake in a tin to pretend it was homemade.

I also have to listen to stories about how they used to lay dead people out on the dining table in the middle of the house so people could walk by. Since I sleep in the dining room in our house, I'm glad things have changed up some—I mean with the dead bodies.

If Big Papa finds a light on when nobody's in a room, he tells us we're 'no account.' He says, "You children will send me to the poorhouse." I thought I already lived there, in the poorhouse. We don't have orange juice for breakfast like most people I spend the night with. Orange juice is considered an 'extra.' In my house that means, we don't buy it.

As soon as I start watching *Rawhide,* my favorite cowboy show, Big Papa gets up and switches off the T.V. It's eight'o'clock. Time for the radio preacher.

Before I fall asleep, I ask Granny to tell me again how she met Big Papa.

"I remember seeing this tall handsome man with red hair and a red handlebar mustache riding his horse down the dirt road toward my house. Your big papa was introduced to my sister at church by a friend of his. He looked at her and whispered, 'She sure is pretty.'"

His friend poked your papa with his elbow, 'You should see her sister!'"

"So that was Big Papa's business, riding his horse down your road that day, to see how pretty you were? You didn't even know he was coming? What if you hated him?" I'm curious.

"I don't know, baby. I introduced him to my mama and daddy and they went in the house. We sat out on the porch swing and visited."

He's the only man I know that had the nerve to change a woman's first and last names. She gets mad as a hornet when you get her on that subject. Granny says her name is Virginia Gertrude. Big Papa says it's Gertrude Virginia and calls her, 'Gertie,' which she hates.

"When he got ready to go that first day, your papa leaned over to kiss me and I turned away. I wouldn't be your grandmother if I had kissed him. After we were married, he told me he wouldn't have come back to see me if I had kissed him, a sure sign I was a loose woman."

## - 6 -

# RUTH SWITCH-A-ROO

"Come here, kids," Daddy calls, as he holds the door open a little. "Are all of you here?"

I'm eleven years old now and I notice he's cleaned up fancier than usual. The white loafers don't go with his dressy blue jacket and gold tie. His eyes have that familiar look after any big event—good or bad, cloudy from too much beer. When I talk to him, I can't tell if he's looking at me.

Daddy's still in the doorway by the time Jimmy and Marilyn get there, and he can't think of what to say, "I didn't have time, I mean we talked about it, but ..." He turns around and talks to somebody. I think I hear a woman's voice. It is. And I smell a woman's perfume mixed in with Daddy's Aqua Velva.

"It was just a spur-of-a-moment thing," he goes on. "Well, Ruth and I slipped off this weekend and got married."

No. This is one of the three things that keep me awake at night. I must have done some mighty big sinning, like that preacher says. I bet Daddy will go off now and live with Ruth.

"I've rented a little house down by the railroad tracks, behind Western Auto. It's a cute little place. We can all live there." Daddy says in his relaxed way.

Marilyn turns around to Jimmy, "I'm not living with Ruth and her five boys. She doesn't even like us. No.!" Marilyn figures, "We need to talk to Big Papa and Granny."

"What?" I realize what's going on. "I'm not going anywhere. Does Granny know? I don't need another mother. Granny's my mother. Granny, come here quick. Daddy's try'n to snatch us!"

"Donna, calm down." Daddy turns and looks back toward the door. "It's okay, Ruth, come on in."

Ruth? Who is this woman? I never laid eyes on this Ruth. The old Ruth is thick with heavy features, weighs more than Daddy. This different Ruth, standing in our living room today, is thin and soft, with sharp features, rosy cheeks, wearing a pink belted dress. This is not the same Ruth he's dated for years. Daddy's gone and done a Ruth switcheroo.

"Hi, children," she says in a soft voice. "I'm Ruth Pixley. It'll take us awhile, I know. I have two boys, John and Dale."

She takes Daddy's hand, "It's okay, Jim. Give us time to get to know each other."

Jimmy turns to Marilyn, "Daddy could have at least told us he was thinking about getting married, and invited us to the wedding before arranging to yank us up and plant us somewhere else."

## Roughneck Daddy: A Memoir

Marilyn realizes, "All my friends pick me up here. They can get me on this phone when I need a ride to school. Daddy's never asked us to move away before. Well, one time we did live in that house near the Catholic church, when Granny was having a hard time with us, but that didn't last long; we were alone too much."

Jimmy decides, "She does look pretty nice, but school is about out. I don't want to move right now. But I don't want to hurt Daddy's feelings. What should we do?"

After Big Papa and Daddy talk a few minutes, Big Papa looks at us, "You children can take your time and decide what you want to do. You're settled here. Your Daddy can come over and see about you until school is out in a few days."

Granny says sometimes I don't pay any mind to what the Lord says to me. But I learned a long time ago to listen to every word my Big Papa says.

I'm scared to leave Granny and Big Papa and go somewhere else to live, even if it is with my Daddy. I know how things go at home now but I'm not sure how it will be with this new Ruth and her boys.

Almost every afternoon, I begin to walk over to the little house on Third Street with Ruth "Switcheroo" and her boys. There's a soft breeze blowing through the window by the red dinette table. Ruth fixes me a baloney sandwich. "Do you want lettuce and cheese?" Then she cuts the soft white bread in half.

Jimmy begins to go with me to play with Dale and John. After Ruth brings him a sandwich, he leans over and whispers to me, "I wanted a mother."

When school is out for the summer, it isn't long before all three of us go every day to see Daddy, Ruth, and the boys.

In the afternoon at three o'clock, the three boys and I go to Western Auto and watch *The Lone Ranger* on a T.V. displayed in their big front window.

When he comes in from the rig one afternoon, Daddy passes us standing in front of the store. He goes out, right then and there, walks in the Western Auto and buys us a television. "I don't want my kids to have to stand in front of a man's place of business to watch their shows."

For a while Daddy brings his paycheck home and doesn't come in drunk. We're a family. I like Ruth's ways. She cooks supper and hugs Daddy when he gets in from the rig, still in his soggy shirt soaked with oil. We all go fishing when he has two days off.

Daddy starts coming in late occasionally from work and Ruth asks, "Where you been, Jim? I smell beer."

"Here's some grocery money, baby. I'm sorry. I had to give one of the men a lift home way out in Marshall," Daddy mumbles.

"Let me know when you'll be late, Jim. Me and the kids worry about you. And you shouldn't be drinking after you get off, when you have to drive those men home. It's dangerous, Jim."

"I said I was sorry, honey. How are the kids? Let's take them out to eat at the Purple Cow tonight. I got a few dollars in my pocket."

"It's late, Jim. They've already eaten. The food's covered up for you on the stove.

"I'll eat it tomorrow night. Get the kids in the car. I'll buy them banana splits."

Dale and John and the three of us all yell, "Yes!" at the same time.

Things start to sound like trouble when Ruth begins to ask for grocery money.

"Where's all the money, Jim? You didn't give me grocery money last week. It's Monday."

"Ruth, goddamnit, you get all the money I've got. Here, I'll give you everything I got in my pocket. Are you satisfied? I don't get paid until Friday.

I stand behind the kitchen door and listen. They fuss about money most of the time now. I'm afraid something bad is going to happen.

I hide behind the kitchen door as usual when they begin to argue.

"Jim," Ruth sounds sad, "I know you're giving money to your old girlfriend, for her five boys. We don't have money to give to those boys. We've got five children here."

Daddy starts to come in drunk every day and every day Ruth wants to know, "Where have you been, Jim, and where's the money?"

"What the hell? If you're not happy, you can get out!" Daddy leaves and slams the door.

Ruth gets quiet.

I figure we're headed back to Big Papa's house soon.

Daddy and Ruth are married a little over a year, when I'm in fifth grade. At the end of that year, I come home from school one day and find that Ruth, John, and Dale are gone. We never see them, or hear from them again.

Big Papa opens the door for us to bring our clothes back into the dining room. Aunt Mellie gave us a little blue chest for our underwear that we find still in the corner. Marilyn gets the top three drawers and I get the bottom two.

I lie in bed that night and decide I'm going to marry a man who loves me, brings his money home, wears a shirt and tie to work, comes home for supper, loves the children, and likes to watch me roll out dumplings on a flour board. I don't want to marry a man who drinks too much. Don't think I'm ever going to forget that.

"Why am I the only one born down here in the South?" I ask my granny.

"Well, Donna, your mother had a hard time with two children, so they moved down here so we could help her; me, your Aunt Mellie, all of us. Your daddy rented the little house right next door where the Thompson's are now. Pretty soon your mama was pregnant again. She found out the new baby would be born around the first week of July so Marion got it in her head that you would be born on Marilyn's sixth birthday, July ninth.

## Roughneck Daddy: A Memoir

She called Dr. Pat that morning, 'This baby has to come today.' But Dr. Pat said, 'Marion, get in a bath, as warm as you can stand it, and drink a bottle of Caster Oil. That baby will come.' He was right."

Marilyn teases me, "You ruined my sixth birthday. I don't think I got any other presents, just a sister."

Every year on July ninth Daddy steals the biggest watermelon he can find from the patch near the rig. He knows it's a good one when he thumps it to hear a hollow sound and turns it over to see a yellow bottom where it sat in the field. I watch his big hands set a green-stripped whopper on a table on the front porch. With Granny's heavy kitchen knife, in only a few whacks, it's laying out red. He slices off the sweetest part and gobbles it up himself. He just can't help it. Nobody asks if we want a birthday cake.

In August I come in from church camp, "Why is this tape on the floor?"

"Stop." Marilyn says, "Your toe's over the line. That's your half."

"Why did you come up with that crazy idea?" I go over and put my foot on the line.

You're always listening in on my conversations. You don't even know how to answer the phone. When Joe called the other day, you told him, 'She's in the bathroom.' That's so embarrassing."

"What's embarrassing about it? Everybody goes to the bathroom."

"Oh, Donna."

"There's one good thing when Marilyn divides our bedroom in half, I can still watch where she hides the key to her diary. Everyday, she writes about Henry Skelton. She sits next to him in band because they both play cornet.

October 17, 1957
Dear Diary,
"Henry's leg touched my leg in band today when we had section rehearsals. This is Wednesday night so I'll see him again at prayer meeting and choir practice afterward. I can't wear my school clothes. Aunt Mellie gave me two corduroy jackets last week one blue and one red. I was really surprised. I can't decide what would be sexy ..."

Sometimes I forget I'm not supposed to know all about her kind-of-pretend, and kind-of- real, boyfriend. There are air plants pinned on the curtains in our windows, every one named Henry Skelton.

"Look, this one has a new plant growing off the side, Marilyn. Don't they have to have water?" I wonder.

"They get water and whatever they need from the air." That would be a good science project for you, Donna," Marilyn says, always thinking about school.

What's worse than half a room is half a bed.

"Get your dirty paws off me." Marilyn says if my sleepy leg finds its way to her side. "You're scratchy. Why don't you shave your legs?" Marilyn is always trying to fix me.

"I'm only eleven years old."

"Oh, well. Stay on your side, will you?" That's the nicest thing that Marilyn can think of to say to me.

After school that afternoon, Marilyn comes to sit next to me and talks sweet. Something's up. "Donna, I'll cook supper tonight if you'll rub my feet and twink my toes."

"What? You cook? Do you know how?" I set things straight.

"Very funny. Come on. I had to march the whole period in band today."

I stay out of the kitchen so I won't have to help. The hamburgers smell good. When we sit down, Marilyn carries the platter stacked with burgers around the table and asks everybody how many they want.

"How many you want, Donna?"

"Two."

"Two! I get the left pointy eyebrow from her.

"Well, I might can eat three." I fail to answer the trick question right once again.

"Oh, Donna." Then I get her disgusted look that makes me feel like I have cooties.

The three of us are scarce on Saturday. Big Papa doesn't believe it's good for a child to sit down even though he never gets up, even to get his iced tea at dinner. He raises his goblet over his head at the table and Granny jumps up. If I stay home I'll have to clean out the rabbit pen or pick peas for Miss Lera.

I spend some Saturday mornings next door helping Mamie clean. It's more fun to clean her house than clean mine. I sit and talk to Mike and make him laugh. "My fat Uncle Lemos puts his belt around him once and then shows me it'll go around me twice, so I'm twice as fat as he is!"

I mention to Mamie that school pictures are the next week. "I'll take you to my beauty parlor, if she'll take you this morning, and get a permanent wave put in that straight hair of yours."

I like my hair.

Mamie stuffs me in the car. On our way there I think about the first time she made me come in from the patch and stuck my head under her kitchen faucet. "Mrs. Fulmer ought to keep your hair clean."

It makes me mad when she talks bad about my granny that way.

In my school picture that year I have a little square of tight curls coming to a point on top of my head.

Mamie's tricks me the same way Marilyn does. She asks me questions she already knows the answers to.

"Donna, do you change your panties every day, baby?"

"Not every day, but pretty regular."

"Oh, Donna," Mamie lets out a deep sigh and flops down on a chair.

That afternoon Big Papa is in a good mood and wants me to snap beans on the front porch with him.

"Big Papa, can I borrow twenty-five cents to go to the show? It's Saturday."

I have to answer the same question each time I 'borrow' money. He asks, "How are you going to pay me back?"

"Daddy will pay you back." I was ready with the right answer.

"Go get my book." Big Papa directs me to his long, skinny black book that sits next to the typewriter. The brown tape curled up on the front doesn't keep the cover on very well. I know why it's about to fall apart, because Big Papa picks it up several times a day to add a quarter or to look down the page at my Daddy's long list of debts.

"I've only got a fifty cent piece so I'll put that down under James' name," he was talking to himself.

Donna Fulmer ......................50 cents (picture show)

Good. I can get popcorn and a Co-Cola.

"Bring back my change." he adds, "You children think I'm made of money. Look at all this money your Daddy owes me. I'll never get it. My-my, you children worry me to death."

A Co-la is ten cents; popcorn, ten cents; gum, five cents. I hope he forgets about the change.

I don't know what's on at the show. I never do. I don't care. I love movies. If I go to a two o'clock, I can walk to the old fire station turned into a movie theater, and get back home before dark.

# Donna F. Orchard

*The Invasion of the Body Snatchers.* I don't like to be scared when I'm by myself, but I have my popcorn box to put over my face today.

That little girl who's running away from the pod trucks looks about my age, about ten years old. I wonder if her mother would hold her hand if she knew her little girl had been taken—was no longer a human being.

The Army men warn people over the radio that the pod trucks look like U.S. military vehicles. "Do not be fooled. May I repeat, do not be fooled. The trucks are on their way to all U.S. cities and even to the small towns."

The pods are ready to snatch bodies when people fall asleep. It looks like there are enough of those pods for a town about the size of Homer. I think I hear something right outside that sounds like those big green army trucks clickity-clacking over the brick streets.

I look around me. The people in these rows look human, but they may be snatched already. How would I know?

"Oh!" A pod person touches my shoulder! My popcorn flies in the air on the person in front of me. I look up and see Daddy.

"Thank God you're here!" Daddy sits down in the seat beside me, takes a deep breath, and tries not to shake when he gives me a long hug.

"You had everybody worried to death, Don. Mama was about to call the police. Nobody knew where you were. I came home from the rig and everybody was looking for you."

"I don't understand. I asked Big Papa for a quarter to come to the show. He must have forgotten. I'm sorry."

"Always tell Granny where you're going, Don. You can't just wander off, baby, without telling anybody. Come on. I got to let Mama know you're okay."

"I just forgot. I promise I won't do that again. Was everybody really worried?" I'm surprised anybody in that house missed me—and a little happy they did. "Can I stay, Daddy?"

"I guess so."

"Stay with me?"

"I can't baby. I just came off the rig. I've got to get some sleep."

"Don't go to sleep, Daddy, the pod ..."

"What did you say, Don?"

"Nothing. Tell Granny, sorry."


When Daddy comes in from the well the next day, he's dirtier than usual, mud all over his neck and in his hair. He takes his pants and shirt off outside on the porch. "Clean that red mud off my boots for me, Don. I've got to get up to the hospital to see about Larry."

"What's wrong with Larry, Daddy? I ask him, "Can I go? How'd ya get all that mud on you?"

"You can't go to the hospital with me this time, Don. Larry's bad off. I don't know if they'll even let me in to see him."

"Is he going to die?"

"No, baby. When we came out on the lease road, it was raining and the planks were washed out. The men were asleep by the time we were down the road a few miles. It was pitch dark and foggy but I thought I saw something white in a ditch. I went on down the road, but thought better of it, so I wheeled around in the middle of the road and went back."

I sit down on the floor by Daddy's feet.

"Sure enough, it looked like our casing crew truck in the ditch. Larry had left the rig a few minutes before we did. I went to get a flashlight and told the men to come help me. They were tired and didn't want to get out of the car. I told them to get their ass out and help me, 'Larry's still in the truck!' I knew it would take all of us."

I thought about my daddy driving the crew home. That could have been him.

"Were Larry's eyes open? Did he know you were there, coming for him, Daddy?"

"I couldn't tell. The men lifted up the cab so I could get the driver's side open and we pulled him out. I tried not to hurt him, but he screamed when I pulled on his legs. His ankle was a mess, bloody, twisted, a raw bone sticking out to one side. He must have fallen asleep at the wheel."

Larry lives right across the street, he ended up being fine and came over when he got out of the hospital. We're all in the living room to hear him tell his story. Right in the middle, he stops and looks at my daddy, "I'll never forget you saved my life, Jim."

## Roughneck Daddy: A Memoir

Before Larry leaves, I hear Big Papa pull him aside, "You're looking at somebody else who wouldn't be here if it wasn't for James."

Daddy jumps in, "Yeah, Papa gets these dizzy spells and he had one while we were in the boat on Mr. Blanton's pond. Fell right out and turned the boat over before I knew it. I looked around and yelled for him, but I didn't see him anywhere. I thought, 'What if I have to go home and tell people my Papa drowned with me right here?' I flipped the boat straight up and there he was under the damn boat."

"Larry, do you want some lemonade and some of my granny's tea cakes?" I ask him as I smile all over because I'm two times proud of my daddy.

# Donna F. Orchard

MARILYN AND DONNA

## - 7 -

# STRAYS

When I hear a knock on the door, my dog, Laddie, jumps up and runs with me too see who it is. I hope that's not somebody who wants my doggie back. A few days ago, Daddy found him in the garden when he almost stepped on him lying there, skinny and hungry. He yelled at me to bring some supper scraps. Granny says Daddy's "soft-hearted to a fault," whatever that means.

If the person at my granny's door wants their dog back, I'll explain he'll have to be dipped for mange every day with stinky sulfur stuff.

"Is this the Fulmer's house?" The stranger looks young, but she has old lady short, curly hair, and has on a long plaid grandmother dress that looks more like a house dress. I decide right off she's weird and I'm not letting her in. We don't often see strangers in Homer; most people who come to the front door are neighbors who walk right in, and if it's dinner time, we put out another plate.

"Yes, Ma'am, this is the Fulmer's house," I tell her.

"You don't have to say ma'am. I'm just fourteen years old."

"You're tall. I'm eleven years old," I say when I forget I'm not going to talk to this oddball.

"I'm Connie Fulmer your second cousin. Is your mama or daddy home?"

"No, but my big papa is."

"Will you go get him, please?" She puts down a bag of stuff in a sack you really couldn't call a suit case.

"Sure, but you'll have to stand right here. Don't come in the door."

I yell, "P a a a pa, somebody's here."

Granny hears me. "Who is it, Donna?"

"Don't know. Never seen her. She's a Fulmer though. Guess she's some kin. You probably know her."

"Hello, may I help you?" Granny goes to the door.

"Hi, Mrs. Fulmer I'm Connie Fulmer from Texas, your second cousin."

"Sure enough. Come in. Who's your mama, baby? I don't believe I know you. Must be from the Huntsville Fulmers. Papa's from Huntsville. We're all kin somewhere down the line."

"Yes, Ma'am, my mama was Sally, but she died when I was born. My daddy's Clyde, but Ma'am, well, he's off in prison, the federal prison near Lufkin. I don't have a way to go see him very often." She looks like she's about to cry.

"I'm sorry. Just a minute. I'll get Papa. Have you had dinner?"

"No, Ma'am. Do you have something cooked? Oh, I mean I wouldn't want to impose." She looks through the screen door and down the hall.

"Well, come on and get some peas and cornbread off the stove. It's still warm."

"Thank you. I'm terrible hungry."

I hide behind the door to hear what Big Papa says; how he gets rid of her. She looks strange as they come. Doesn't look like any Fulmer I've ever seen.

Big Papa comes in the back door dirty from the garden, "What can we do for you, young lady?"

"Hello, Mr. Fulmer. I'm Connie Fulmer, a cousin from Texas."

Papa asks, "Now who is your daddy over there in Texas? My folks were originally from Huntsville."

"Clyde." She says, but it sounds phony to me. I don't know any relations named Clyde.

Granny taps Big Papa and whispers, "He's in prison."

"Who was your granddaddy?" Big Papa continues to try to figure this thing out.

"I don't know. He died before I was born."

"Clyde ..., I don't think I know that strain of Fulmers. What are you doing over here by yourself, little lady?" Papa looks puzzled.

"After Daddy got sent away, they told me his brother, Sam, in Mississippi, could take me. I had enough money for a Greyhound and went over there to Picayune. He and Doris said they couldn't do it, could barely feed their own. They gave me enough money to get back this far. Now I'm stranded." Joe Friday would never fall for that story, I thought. She was finishing one plateful of peas and cornbread and glancing up at the stove.

"I see, well, wait right here and let me talk to Gertie."

Papa takes me by surprise when he comes back, "Young lady, you can stay here a day or two until you can get somebody in Texas. You can use our telephone there in the hall to call some of your kin."

Even if she had kin, she's probably worn out her welcome with them, eaten all their peas and cornbread already.

She tells Papa, "I'll try to call Texas tomorrow. Thank you, sir."

Granny sees her glancing around and asks her if she wants dessert, some cornbread and honey. She takes dessert and more sweet tea too.

Big Papa calls me, "Donna, where are you? Can this young lady sleep with you a couple of nights while Marilyn's away at band camp?"

"No way! Marilyn's bad enough. I'm not sleeping with some outsider."

Papa comes back in the breakfast room, "Connie, you can sleep on the couch in the living room. Donna will fix some sheets on there and give you a pillow off her bed."

I thought Granny would have learned her lesson about strays that morning when the three of us showed up at her door. We've been here nine years now.

Two nights with Connie turn into four. I mostly stay away from her stories about how she can break a horse and then ride him in a rodeo. I suppose she breaks those horses in a dress since that's all she wears.

# Roughneck Daddy: A Memoir

I'm about to fall asleep when she comes in and sits on my bed. "Come here, Donna. I want to talk to you. Let's go in the living room." She gets real close and whispers in my ear, "Have you ever done it with a boy?"

"Gosh, no. I already told you, I'm only eleven years old."

"You're tall like me. You look about twelve years old, Donna. Anyway, you need to know this—it hurts. It'll cause you pain and you bleed and bleed."

"What? I don't want to bleed! In the movies boys and girls talk about it. Then after a lot of smooching they plan to get alone to do it, like it's fun. I don't believe you."

"When he sticks the thing in, it tears you up inside and blood goes everywhere—don't ever do it."

Things go topsy-turvy, and I feel dizzy like I'm going to throw up. "But I want to marry a man some day and have babies. I love little babies," I say as tears roll down my cheeks.

"That hurts too. Grown-up people hide all this from you." Connie continues, pleased I'm brought to tears.

I run away to Granny's room feeling mixed up. I thought doing it was fun. When Daddy gets off the job, he can't wait to clean up, put on Aqua Velva and go see his girlfriend, the first Ruth. I figure they do it.

I respect my Granny too much to tell her exactly what this Connie told me, but the next morning, I tell her enough.

Papa contacts somebody by telephone, buys Connie a bus ticket and puts her on a Greyhound back to Texas a couple of days later.

## Donna F. Orchard

It's a good thing Granny let me in when I showed up and let me stay, because now I'm almost twelve years old and she needs me. I sleep with her and help her to the bathroom during the night; I go get her Bible for her in the next room; and I give her a sponge bath before she goes to the doctor.

Laddie finally gets well from the mange and he's my best buddy for a long time.

# Roughneck Daddy: A Memoir

MARION DENTON

*Come on down to the mermaid café*
*And I will buy you a bottle of wine*
*And we'll laugh and toast to nothing*
*And smash our empty glasses down.*
*Let's have a round for these streets and those soldiers,*
*A round for these friends of mine.*
*Let's have another round for the bright red devil…*

*Joni Mitchell*

# - 8 -

# TOE DANCER

Homer, Louisiana

September 8, 1953

Hello Marion,

The children are back in school. Marilyn went to band camp at Corney Lake this summer.

Marion we haven't said anything to the children about you. I suggest you come and be with them more and let them know you better.

Mother and Dad told me to tell you to come. I will see that you have the things you need.

We don't want to keep the children away from you. I don't tell them what to do and what not to do. I leave them alone. They have their own thoughts.

Mother loves you better than you will ever know. The things you did for her while you were here were never forgotten.

Come on down Marion we will try to make you happy as you once were.

I know you will enjoy the children. Will be looking to hear from you and seeing you before long.

Jim

# Donna F. Orchard

Along with this invitation from Daddy in long hand, was a typed letter from Big Papa on his old Packard typewriter that always needed a ribbon.

In the morning before school, Jimmy and I go out front to play Mumblety Peg while Marilyn finishes dressing.

"I call first flip." As I press the handle of the pocket knife to my head and flip it into the sand, I see something out of the corner of my eye. A woman in a fancy black and white flowered dress walks right up in the yard, her arms open wide, "Hi, honey."

I whisper to Jimmy. "Who's that?"

"It's Mother, stupid. I didn't know she was coming. I don't think Daddy knows," Jimmy looks worried, "maybe she brought some of my toys."

"Oh, my gosh! I sort of remember now. How long we been here, Jimmy?"

"I don't know, Donna, lots of years."

"Jimmy and Donna, come here. Let me look at you." Mother grabs us.

I try to squirm away, and blurt out, "What are you doing here?"

"Why, I'm here to see you, baby. Come give me a hug. I can't believe you're eleven years old, Donna. And Jimmy you're fifteen now and such a tall boy."

"We have to leave for school in ten minutes," Jimmy says, "Mike, next door, gives us a ride. Does Granny know you're here?"

"No, I got to the hotel late last night. Is Daddy home?"

"He's at work. He went in last night at twelve and he'll work out at twelve noon. Wait just a minute," Jimmy says, as he runs inside.

"Donna, I've got lots to talk to you about," Mother turns and puts her arm around me. "I brought my scrapbook with all of your baby pictures. I even have a picture of you and Mamie's little black BB dog. I guess she still names all her dogs, BB dog," she giggles.

I guess I feel happy to see my mother, but it also makes me sad and afraid for some reason. I'm used to living with Granny, Big Papa and Daddy; in a way I don't want her to show up and poke her nose into my life. I hope she doesn't ever finds out I have those thoughts. I don't want to hurt her feelings. She has already changed things by showing up and she should have told us she was coming. I thought it would be for Marilyn's graduation next year. I feel bad because I just want her to leave me alone.

I'm getting along fine without a mother. None of my friends know her and I'm embarrassed to tell them she's here. Daddy told me she drinks. She can't drink around here because our town doesn't sell booze. None of my friends spend the night because I know Daddy might come in drunk, now I have to worry about my mother.

She may have brought some whiskey with her. I hope she doesn't make a scene. She's loud like me. People always tell me to calm down. I don't want to calm down, why should I? That's one thing I like about mother; she's fun and likes to tell stories, holds her head back and laughs like I do. And I have her pretty legs and I'm a good dancer.

I'm glad she came.

Jimmy sees Big Papa in the hall, "Guess who's here, Papa? Our Mother is here from Cincinnati. She walked right up in the yard. Did you know she was coming? Does Daddy know she's here?"

Papa turns to find Granny, "No son, I invited your mother to come for a visit in a letter some months back, but I didn't know she was coming today. Tell Marion to come in and make herself at home."

Jimmy yells back, "Mother's staying down at the hotel and I'm going to spend the day with her."

Big Papa steps outside, "Welcome, Marion."

"Thank you, Mr. Fulmer" She sounds friendly, but she doesn't hug Big Papa. In fact, I can't think of anybody who hugs Big Papa.

"How are you, Marion?" Granny runs out smiling, in her green house dress with pink flowers, and gives

Mother a long hug. "We've missed you, Marion. The kids have missed you. You are still so beautiful."

"I'm thrilled to see the children. They look all grown up, so tall and grown up," Mother gushes. "Where's Marilyn?"

"She's still primping for school. M a a a r r i lyn, come out here," I yell.

"We're glad you're here to see the children, Marion. I guess you got my letter inviting you to come down for a visit," Big Papa opens the door for her to come in. "We want them to know you. They need you, Marion."

"We'd love to have you stay with us but we don't have an extra bed," Granny apologizes.

"I have a room at the hotel around the corner for a few days, Mrs. Fulmer. I'll be fine."

Big Papa turns to Jimmy, "Son, you're already having trouble in school this year in Mrs. Linton's room. You can visit with your mother this afternoon when you get home. She'll be here for several days. Now you go on to school today."

"But, Papa!" Jimmy's face is red, he's so mad. "Please, Big Papa," Now he's about to cry.

"Go on, son, like I tell you." Papa's mind is made up.

You can bet Marilyn will want to go to school. She rushes out the door still putting her sweater on, "Hi, Mother. Jimmy ran in to tell me you were here. We'll come see you at the hotel after school or you can come back here. I've got to get an article in for the school newspaper today."

"You're so beautiful, honey. Give me a hug. You write, Marilyn?"

"Yeah," Marilyn nods, "I'm the editor of our junior high newspaper."

"I'm so proud of you. Can't you and Jimmy stay with me today? I haven't seen you in so long," Mother says in a sad voice.

Big Papa says to Mother, "The baby can go with you, Marion. The other two need to be in school. They have their routine. They didn't know you were coming today. James will be in from the rig about one o'clock. I know he'll want to see you, and Marion, come back to see us any time while you're here."

"I understand, Mr. Fulmer." Mother slumps her shoulders as she turns around and gives up, just like she had to give up when we were taken away from her. I'm mad at Big Papa for treating Mother like a visitor. She is our mother. "Come on, Donna. I'll see Jimmy and Marilyn this afternoon."

I stare at Mother; look her up and down—three strands of pearls at her neck, big white earrings, hose and high heels. When I hug her, she smells like talcum powder and sweet perfume. I decide she's much more of a girly girl than I am.

Mother looks next door, "I want to go see Mamie and Mike while I'm here. When you were a baby, it tickled Mamie to see you all dressed up in the morning after I gave you a bath."

We go around by the huge old oak in the front yard to see the orange tulips and full yellow daffodils in

Granny's sunny bed on the side. Mother turns back to look straight up in the tree that shades the whole front yard and says how much she loves it.

"I almost died under that big tree."

"What, Donna? What did you say, honey? Don't try to scare me. What happened?"

"A hunk of steak. Nobody noticed when I ran from the table. I couldn't breathe. I thought I was a goner, but before I stopped breathing, I gave it one more big cough and the meat shot straight out onto the grass."

"Oh, Donna, be careful, slow down, and chew your food."

"Don't worry. I'm okay."

I can't stop looking at her. I think Marilyn looks like Mother with her dark curly hair.

I don't favor her at all. I have blond hair, if it's not summer, in which case my hair's green from the swimming pool, and red freckly skin. All of us have our mama's black eyes.

"Come walk with me around to the hotel, sweetheart, and we'll spend the day together."

"There are forty-seven cracks in the street from here to the corner and a hundred and one lines on the sidewalk."

"You must play out here every day. What do you play?"

"Anything, hopscotch, kick the can, or baseball that doesn't count; only games in the patch count. I'll show you." Running around the bases, "Miss Lee's grass is first, the sewer cover is second, and Miss Lera's grass is third. Our sidewalk is home."

"Looks like fun, honey."

"Only thing is, sometimes cars come and we have to get off the street. They come up the hill and just drive right over our field in the middle of a game."

"Lots of kids in the neighborhood?"

"All boys: Bobby, Billy, Ronnie, Perry, and of course Bubba—my nickname for Jimmy.

I call to her, "Mother, cross over here to this side with me." When she's back walking beside me, I tell her where everything is in Homer. "That's the Campbellite Church. They're kind of weird. Don't use instruments when they sing. And over there, that's Shorty's gas station. That's where Daddy hangs out and sometimes and gets gas. He has Fire Balls in that machine for a penny. The big church across the street with the white pillars in front, that's the Baptist Church, my church."

"You don't go to Catholic mass? Well, of course not."

Oh, I shouldn't have said that. Granny told me we were all baptized when we were babies and Daddy promised to raise us Catholic. But the only baptizing I remember is the one I got across the street at my Baptist church when I was nine years old.

"Why don't you rent a room in Miss Rae's motel down the hill from our house? That's where Uncle Lemos and Aunt Sugar stay."

"They charge close to six dollars a night, Don; it's cheaper here at the hotel."

I hope Brother Hall, my preacher, doesn't look across the street and see me go in this nasty place. Granny tells me not to go near this hotel, and to look straight ahead when I walk by. Old men sit on the stoop during the day, smoking cigarettes and make a point to look up and stare at me when I go past.

Mother and I begin to climb to her third floor room on a dark narrow path that feels creepy. We get to room 301 at the top of the stairs. At least we can run down fast if anybody bothers us.

The floor is clean, but I smell cigarettes. A small table is covered with a white lace scarf, Granny would say, needs some bleach.

"Have some nosh, baby." I hurry over to the long coffee table ready to eat the snacks we rarely have at home. After getting there in breakneck speed, I decide the food must have been out all night: limp potato chips, stale crackers, hard pieces of cheese, and more of those dry little cookies we get in the mail from Cincinnati.

It feels funny at first, when I sit by mother, when she reaches over and rubs my arm or brushes my bangs out of my face, like she does it every day. I like it.

"Tell me about school, Donna. What do you like best?"

"We do work all day, unless it's recess. When the bell rings I'm so ready to get outside with the girls or with Harold, Harold, Whiskey Barrel."

"Who?"

"Harold. He's a crazy boy in my class. Lives right over the hill from my best friend, Annie Roonie. Sometime if we want to be scared, we go up the hill and yell his name, then run back down and hide behind the catalpa tree."

"What do you do when you get home? Do your homework or go out to play?"

"Marilyn reads. To me that's the same thing as doing homework. Bubba and I play ball. I mean Jimmy. On the weekends, Granny sometimes lets me walk across the bridge about a mile over to Annie Roonie's house. She never comes to my house. Nobody comes to my house to play or spend the night. Daddy is usually sleeping and we have to be quiet. Anyway, our house is already filled up with people. Big Papa says we don't need extras. I call Annie's mother when I'm on my way and she watches for me. Her Granny lives out in the country and we sometime stay out there a week or two in the summer. She cleans the fish we catch, even if they're minnows, and fries them up. We go out in the woods and smoke rabbit tobacco or ride her horse, Maude."

"Smoke, what? You two little girls find cigarettes?"

"No it's just a weed. Don't worry. I'd get kicked out of the house if Big Papa found out I smoked a cigarette. Anyway, I'm afraid of horses and Maude knows it. That old horse becomes a stallion when I get on, gallops into every creek she can find, to give me a good soaking, then hopes to shake me off and stomp me to death, me just a yellin' for her to stop. When Annie Roonie says, 'Let's ride the horse,' she knows what she's stirring up."

Mother walks across the room to the counter to make ham sandwiches. Her legs are long and beautiful when she kicks up the bottom of the silky dress. Daddy says she's a knockout in high heels.

# Roughneck Daddy: A Memoir

"As soon as you're old enough to ride the bus, I want you to come see me in Cincinnati. We'll get your Uncle Benny's kids to come over to my place every day."

"Is Cincinnati a big city? I want to go now. I like big cities. Well, I've never actually been to one, just Shreveport on the way to Lake Bistineau. Marilyn keeps begging Daddy to take her to Shreveport to the skin doctor over there to get some medicine for the bumps on her face. He doesn't have time." I sit by Mother on the couch and twirl her blue and silver jangle bracelet round and round on her arm.

"I'll talk to Jim about that," Mother frowns. "Maybe Jimmy and Marilyn will come with you to Cincinnati. It's a long trip, Don, about twenty-two hours; you have to stop at the Post Houses along the way to use the restroom." Mother puts her arm around me and pulls me to her.

"Ouch! Don't hug me so tight."

"I'm sorry, honey ... uh ... let's look at these pictures."

We sift through the faded yellow photo album, jam-packed: black pages lined with pictures of the three of us, the Virgin Mary on the front of a Christmas card, Mother and her girlfriends dressed up in hats and gloves, a wine list of their favorite drinks, a handsome old boyfriend smoking a cigar, Mother in a show with a long feather coming out of her cap, letters from priests, autographs of famous people I've never heard of.

"Who is Marion Denton?"

"That's me, Don. That was my show name. Denterclausen was too long for the playbills."

"You had a show name? Like movie stars? I don't think anybody in Homer has a show name."

I see that Mother saved every card we sent her over the years. "I couldn't print my name very good on this Christmas card. I don't remember that one. Want to see how good I print now? I'll show you later." I turn the page. "Here's you and Daddy holding one of us."

"That's in D.C., Don. That's Marilyn."

"Daddy is so dressed up, white shirt, pants, and even white shoes. He still has some white loafers. You look tall, and skinny, and pretty."

"That's three weeks after Marilyn was born, a picture of our first baby to send to the family."

"I can tell you both wanted to hold Marilyn for the picture, so you shared her.

"Your Daddy loves babies."

"He still asks mothers if he can hold their babies. I run away when he starts that. Women don't want to hand off their babies to anybody on the street who stops them to brag about their cute baby." I turn a page in the album, "Here you are in a short feathery skirt. One foot on the floor and the other leg stretched up until your toe touches your head—the sideway splits."

"I started dance lessons when I was four and I loved it. Dancing was all I ever wanted to do. Then at fourteen years old, about Marilyn's age, I went to New York to live with my sister, Peg, who worked there. I left with a few costumes made by my mother, determined to get in some of the big shows."

"Your mama let you leave home? Weren't you scared?"

"No because Peg was in New York. I don't think she would have let me go alone."

"Were you a toe dancer?"

"Yes" she says slipping off her shoes. "Take your finger and feel the tips of my toes, baby."

"Oh, my gosh, the ends of your toes are flat!"

"That's from balancing up in the air in my ballerina slippers all those years."

"Were they pink?"

"Sometimes, or white, with ribbons tied up the ankles. I have foot pain every day now, Don, because of a dancing career. If I have to wait a while for a cross town bus, I take my heels off and stand in my stocking feet."

"Mother, did you ever teach me how to dance, how to point my toes or anything?"

"You were so young, Don. I taught Jimmy and Marilyn some tap steps, got them up and taught them a few little routines."

"I might have been a ballerina like you. I pick up steps real fast. Want to watch me jitterbug. Here I go … its better with music and a partner. Did you see how I can cross my arms over my knees? Daddy taught me that."

"Your Daddy's a good dancer. We both loved to jitterbug." She pulls me close, "I can't believe you're here with me."

## Donna F. Orchard

When Mother goes to the kitchen, I look on the dresser at the pink hand cream and beside it, a yellow bottle of perfume. I spray some on my arm.

"What do I smell?" Mother hands me a soft drink.

"I don't know. Mother, how did you meet Daddy, anyhow, when you lived in Cincinnati and Daddy grew up down here in the South?"

"I met Jim in Washington, D.C., right at the end of the Great Depression. He was up there to find work. Your Daddy's a wonderful cook, Don. He was the chef at the Heidelberg Hotel, at their German restaurant. I came in every day for lunch. He made me laugh the first time I met him, one of his crazy stories. He said he could hear my laugh all the way in the kitchen when I came in the hotel."

I notice that mother's earrings are blue and silver to match her bracelet.

"The hotel had a brown mahogany bar that wrapped halfway around the dance floor. Oh, honey, your daddy was the most handsome man in the world! He had thick brown hair and green eyes. My mother didn't like him, thought he was a country bumpkin. But I did. He was a strong Southern boy, different from anybody I had ever met."

"What's a country bumpkin?" Mother throws back her head and laughs loud.

"A country boy. Anybody—not from Cincinnati. I'd hang around the hotel until Jim got off and we'd jitterbug. Then the reeds and brass swayed side to side as we danced to the last slow one. He carried my heels and walked me to my apartment close by. In less than a year, we were married."

"What church did you get married in?" I walked in the kitchen where mother opened up a can of potato salad. I didn't know you could buy potato salad in a can. We talked while she made liverwurst sandwiches and ate at the white dinette table. What is liverwurst?

"We went to the crowded downtown courthouse in D.C. to get married, with just Peg, my sister, and Flo, my sister-in-law, as witnesses. There was a long line of people waiting to get their car tags just outside the glassed-in office where we said our vows. All those people watched as we said, 'I do.' When we were leaving, a woman stepped out of line, tears streaming down her face, to hug us and wish us well, in Spanish. It was one of those unforgettable moments." She roars with laughter as she swishes across the room, her dress rippling as she walks in her high heel sandals and we sit back on the couch.

"I'll never love another man like I do your daddy." Then she starts to cry.

"He says the same thing about you."

What could have messed them up? Why did she leave us alone in the park if she loved us so much? Why didn't she come to get us? She could have found a house and lived in Homer near us. If somebody tried to take my babies, I'd find them, and sit on the curb until they sent my babies out—for as long as it took...

I look at a picture of Mother and Daddy together in the album. "You're about as tall as Daddy, aren't you, Mother?"

"No, not quite. I'm five feet eight inches tall and he's six feet one."

"I have your pretty long legs, but I'm taller than all the boys in fifth grade."

"They'll catch up one day, hon; you're my beautiful baby." she squeezed me.

"One good thing is that the boys let me play baseball with them."

I think Mother is drinking A&W Root Beer too, but after lunch she starts slurring her words like on the telephone. I wonder where she found beer or whiskey in Homer. She starts crying a lot and hugging me too much.

"Here's a list of your shows, Mother. You were in Washington, Idaho, Utah, Wyoming, Colorado."

"Seven nights a week, Donna. But, I was young then. It was an exciting life, all of the applause. When we joined Chorus Equity they were forced to give us a night off."

"Why did you stop dancing?"

"My feet, but the business changed, too. When the talkies hit the theaters, live reviews were on their way out. *Rio Rita* was my last big show. A wealthy tycoon bought out RKO, the company I worked for, and made it into a movie company, those sonsofbitches."

There's a knock on the door and I see that it's my Daddy home from work. This is the first time I've ever seen my mother and daddy together. They hug, and at first I feel good when they smile, and seem glad to see each other.

"How have you been, Marion?" Daddy asks as he stands in his usual swagger with his left foot out.

"I've been okay, Jim. I'm cleaning houses. It's pretty good money. You wouldn't believe the crap I have to take off these rich women. I've walked out on a few of them."

"How's Benny, Gerri, and the kids?"

"They're fine. You wouldn't believe how big those kids are now. Ted's almost six feet tall."

Out of nowhere Mother says, "Your mother wanted these kids all along, Jim."

"What Mar …?"

"How do you think I felt when I came home to that empty house, my babies gone? I cried for days. Didn't get out of bed."

"Don't start with me, Marion; I didn't know what else to do. I had to work. I feel bad about taking the kids away from you. I know you love them. They need their mother.

We wanted all three of these children, Marion, so happy every time you got pregnant. But when Jimmy had his accident, after school, at four o'clock when he should have been home, I got scared. He fell off the slide and cut his chin open, bleeding. The school couldn't find you, Marion. They called me at Kroger's and I took him to the hospital. The kids told me you were so nervous they had to stay outside all day. I understand you were sick, but …"

"I'm not sick. That was just an excuse to get my babies."

"Okay. Okay, Marion. Let's not go over all that again. It never gets us anywhere. Just try to have a nice visit with the children. I know they've missed you. You'll always be their mother."

Mother starts to yell, "She's glad to get me out of the picture. She never liked me anyway. That was a shitty thing to do to me, to steal my babies. You Southern bastards had it all planned. You were even friends with the judge. I could never get my babies back, you bast …"

"Chrissake, Marion, I had to have help with these kids. You came down here to start some shit. I should have known it."

I start to cry and run out the door to sit on the stairs, but I can still hear them yelling.

"I tell you what, get your goddamn stuff and I'll take you to the bus station. Right now! And don't ever come back here upsetting these children, Marion, They don't want to hear your bullshit."

"Don't… Jim." I can hear Mother crying.

"I said get your goddamn stuff. I knew you'd come down here and cause trouble. That's the reason I waited so long to tell you to come."

"Don," Daddy stuck his head out the door. "Go walk back to your granny's, baby."

I know she's going to leave. In a way, I'll be relieved. I have enough to worry about. I don't want to be on pins and needles wondering when they'll have another fight. I sit down on the curb and cry.

## Roughneck Daddy: A Memoir

When Jimmy got home from school, he ran in the door and found me in the back. I could see his eyes were swollen, that he had been crying. "Where's Mother, Donna? Where's Mother?"

"Mother and Daddy had a fight. He took her to the bus station."

"I knew it! I knew it!" he screamed. "I told Mr. Tanner she wouldn't be here. Nobody believed me."

Granny calls out, "Jimmy," Her voice sounds serious so I stand behind the corner and listen. "Come here, son. I can tell your eyes are red and puffy. Mrs. Linton phoned to see if you were okay. She said you cried all day at school. I'm so sorry, son. When you couldn't tell her why you were upset, she said she sent you to the principal. What did Mr. Tanner say to you, honey?"

"He just let me sit in his office because I was crying. I told him I wanted to stay home with my mother."

"I told your teacher about the situation. She was worried about you, Jimmy, said you are usually quiet, and she hardly knows you're in the room."

"Anyway," he said, "I wanted to ask Mother if she got my letters. I sent her two letters a long time ago to ask her to send some of my toys and my glove."

"Come on Bubba" I say, "let's go to Shorty's station and get a Dreamcicle."

"I don't feel like it."

Granny hugs Jimmy and the three of us stand in the hall crying.

# - 9 -

# BLOW OUT

I turn twelve years old before the fall of 1959, the first year I have Miss Hightower for English. Jimmy and Marilyn tell me if I'm not a rule follower already, I'll become one soon.

When she gives my English diagnostic back on the second day of class, she asks me sideways, "You're not Marilyn Fulmer's sister are you?"

"Yes, Ma'am." When I answer, I swear I hear her gasp.

"What grade is she in now?"

"She's a senior, on the yearbook staff."

"Oh, well, maybe she can help you with your semicolons, Donna. She was such an excellent student, excellent. She was my assistant, graded papers and tutored for me in the afternoons. Writes beautifully."

"Yes, Ma'am." Gee whiz.

School gives me a headache. My routine in the afternoons is to do my homework in five minutes because I know it all ( or if I don't know it all, I get to school early the next day and copy somebody's), then grab my glove and go down to the patch and play baseball until Granny makes me come in after dark.

Today, I'm busting out the screen door for the patch when Granny asks me to pick some green apples in the back yard and pare them for a cobbler. It takes a thousand because they're little ole things. I had been at it since I got in from school when I smell oil before I see Daddy start up the back steps. He takes off his boots on the landing and stands in the breakfast room where I'm working. The only thing I can see are his green eyes; his face, arms and neck are smeared brown and greasy.

"You better go on and back out, Daddy. Granny's going to have a hissy fit if you come in the house like that. What happened? My lord, I've never seen oil all over you like that!"

"Get me some pants and an old rag, baby. Be careful with these nasty clothes when you put them in the washing machine. Wash 'em by themselves, Don."

"I know." Now I've got grease all over me just going to the washing machine.

"I got some of this shit off in the dog house, washed my mouth out," Daddy sounded worn out. "I didn't want to swallow that nasty mess. Tried to clear out my ears, about all I had time to do. The inside of my car is plain ruined, hauling the guys. I made a break for it before one of those worms lit up a cigarette and blew the whole place to hell."

"Your hair even looks slick. Here, Daddy, wash it with Tide. That works,"

I hand Daddy his an old pair of sweat pants and a rag and he uses the hose in the back yard to get the worst off, while I sit on the stoop patiently because

I knew he was about to tell a good story with all the details.

"I was up in the derrick and I heard a rumble down in the hole. I don't think the driller realized, when he heard the kick, what was happening. Before I had time to yell down, there was a flash, and then a blast jarred my feet off my board. The well was gonna go."

"Did anybody get killed?"

"One man got burned pretty bad, third degree, Don. I reached out to cling onto one of the steel shafts, when I was knocked from one side to the other in that derrick. Thank God I didn't have a damn safety belt on 120 feet up there. Sounded like a freight train when we hit that gas. I leaned out and pulled the soft line close. Had to get ready to leap out on the damn thing. I hung there seemed like forever while that rope swung me back and forth, banged me up against the derrick. I pushed away with one foot until I could get my legs around the rope to slide down. The whole shebang was about to blow."

Daddy shook his head, "I was flying down that rope by the time my feet touched the ground. Looked up to see the goddamn tubing bust clean off. Oil went spewing everywhere, shot way high in the air. It felt like hail until I looked down and saw grease plastered all over me. We fell over each other trying to get away. After we jumped in the car, we looked around at each other, 'What in the shit just happened?'"

"Are you hurt, Daddy?"

"I'm okay, but look at my arms; they're already red and burning. I don't ever want to be caught up in that derrick again when some goddamn driller isn't paying attention. Or maybe he'd never seen a well come in. I won't ever work for him again. You can get fuckin' killed. Honey, I've got to hurry up and get in the tub. Find my lye soap and Petroleum Jelly. Some of the hands got that foul stuff down in their throats. Their lips swelled, burned, and they were already having a hard time swallowing," he hollered on his way in to take a bath.

I keep knocking on the bathroom door, "Are you okay, Daddy?"

"I got to get all this mess off of me. Tell Jimmy to come here and help me with my back, Donna. I'll be finished in a minute. Get a Q-tip, Don, and see if you can see any black goo inside my ears. I can feel something like water in my ears. I want to loosen up every bit of that stuff and get it out."

"Tell me if I'm sticking this thing too far." I ask hoping I don't bust his ear drum.

"Swab it around. See, that's oil, that thick reddish stuff," he said.

"I can still smell it, Daddy."

"I'll have to bathe a couple of times to get all this grease off. I hope you kids don't come down with something from these fumes. Did ya'll start to school this week, Don?"

"Yeah, my teacher's already asked me if I'm Marilyn's sister."

"Uh-oh."

"I don't know what's wrong with having a 'C' reputation. That's average, isn't it? I admit I don't like to do homework."

"You'll be alright, baby. You always are."

Daddy asks Marilyn, "After I eat do you want to play some five card draw, Sis?"

"Sure, as soon as I sew these pleats in my skirt. I want to wear it tomorrow," Marilyn says as she peddles the sewing machine while pushing the red plaid under the needle.

"Donna you ought to learn how to sew. Didn't you take home economics?" Daddy teases me. He knows I did—one of those trick questions that Marilyn uses on me. "Your

Granny thinks all your teachers have got old since they taught Marilyn, too old to teach—because Marilyn made A's and you make C's. Then Daddy busts out laughing.

"You want to learn to play poker, Donna?" A trick question from Marilyn.

"Nope. Too much like math for me. I'll watch." I shoot back.

"You deal, Sis. Okay, ante up. Each straw is a dollar." Daddy explains.

"Two," Daddy says.

"I'll see that and raise you two," Sis answers.

"Let me peek at what you have," I say hanging around Daddy's neck. "Oh, Marilyn you might as well fold your hand."

"Shut up, Donna. You don't know what I have, you little twerp."

"How many cards do you want, Daddy?" Marilyn deals.

"I'll take two." He's got a plan.

"Why do you do that?" I ask Daddy.

"What?" he looks at me as he takes tobacco out of his pocket.

"Roll your own cigarettes." I've always wanted to know.

"Cause the damn things got too high." He takes out a thin little white paper, licking it from one end to the other, until it's good and wet, pouring the Prince Albert in the middle. Then folding the soggy paper over, he smashes the end every which way until the cigarette comes to a funny-looking point. Flattening the other end, he sticks the thing in his mouth right quick, then flips his Zippo lighter with the pointer dog on the front, raises his head as he lights up, and takes a long, satisfying draw.

"Who cares, Donna," Marilyn fusses. "Stop asking so many questions. We're in the middle of a game."

Marilyn whines. "Okay, you want to bet or fold, Daddy?"

"I'll go two," he says

"I think you're bluffing. I'll see you and raise you five," Marilyn sounds confident.

"I'll see your five and raise you two," he says.

Marilyn calls, "I got two pair."

"I got three of a kind," Daddy gee-haws.

"Oh, man!" Marilyn owns up.

"Don't give your hand away with your eyes, Sis. Don, Sis thinks she can beat her daddy at poker."

On Saturday morning early I hear, Big Papa's voice. "You children come here, all three of you."

Today's the day. I always thought I would live past twelve years old.

A few weeks ago my red crayon got dull when working on a science project, so I walked over to Big Papa's pencil sharpener. It must be one of the first ones ever made. Screwed into the wall in Daddy's room, all the yellow plastic's turned pea green, cracked all the way around. I put the crayon in and stared to grind. The dang thing broke off! I tried to fish it out every which way with tweezers and everything, but it broke off too short down in there to get. I wasn't in the mood that day for a long sermon from Big Papa about what a hopeless, low down individual I had become, who doesn't deserve to breathe the same air he does.

Marilyn knows something's wrong with me. For a week I haven't been able to sleep, tossing and turning while trying to stay on my side of the bed. "If you won't tell me what's wrong, just go sleep on the couch so you don't touch me with your grimy paws and keep me awake."

I come close to confiding in Marilyn and telling her about the pencil sharpener since I'm terrified, but then I calm myself down with this thought: Big Papa might die before he ever has to sharpen his pencil again.

He didn't. When I hear his tone of voice, calling all three of us that morning, I knew that he had finally tried to sharpen a pencil.

As we line up in the breakfast room, "Which one of you children stuck a Crayola in my pencil sharpener and left it stuck all up in there so I can't even sharpen my pencil?"

I look straight down at the floor because I know Marilyn's gonna look at me and say something stupid like, "Big Papa, you know it was Donna. Donna, tell him the truth so we can go."

But she doesn't. Marilyn says, "I didn't do it."

Jimmy says, "Well, I sure didn't."

My turn, "Big Papa, you know I would have told you if I'd done it."

"All three of you are going to stand here until somebody tells me the truth," Big Papa says as he watches all three of us.

I stand on one foot and then the other it seems like forever until Jimmy says, "This isn't fair Big Papa, I didn't do anything."

Marilyn chimes in, "Me either."

"That goes for me too," I can feel my face turning red.

"Why do you children want to worry an old man like this?" Big Papa gets tired of standing there too, "Go on. I can't believe nary a thing you say anyway. You kids are no account."

## Roughneck Daddy: A Memoir

Later when Jimmy jerks me up by my collar to make me confess, I stick to my story right on. I figure it'll be safe to tell him the truth when we sit in our rocking chairs, when I'm about eighty years old and Jimmy's eighty-four. The radio preacher says we better come clean before we meet our Maker.

I hope this doesn't cause Big Papa to have one of his spells. Nobody else seems to worry, but I stay awake until he decides to get back in bed and go to sleep. Granny doesn't know what to do for him. He stays awake for two or three days in his brown rocker with the shotgun in his lap. "Guess I should go ahead and blow my brains out." Daddy says Big Papa's just trying to get attention. But I stay awake in case he has a mind to do it. I lie there and work out what I'll do if I hear the blast.

But, Miss Lera's husband across the street really does do it. Mr. Landrum, president of the bank, is late coming home one night so Miss Lera calls the sheriff to go check on him. They find him in the vault with a bullet in his head. Now anytime her name is mentioned on the front porch, somebody's sure to say, "That poor Miss Lera. You remember her husband blew his brains out in the bank." Marilyn goes over to spend the night with her sometime, to keep her company. I go if Marilyn doesn't want to. I like the smell of her Dial soap. When I grow up, I'm going to keep plenty of Dial soap.

As I've mentioned, I skeedattle from our dark house every chance I get. My voice is deep and strong like all the Fulmers who can do three part harmony. I can sing. Uncle Ezzie, Big Papa's brother, picks me up Sunday nights when he goes to lead a 'singing' in some little country church.. My cousin Alexis and I who are both twelve. get all dressed up to sing a duet, the special music after the offering plate is passed.

When Uncle Ezzie picks us up, we have to crawl into the back seat, but you've got to understand something about his old black Ford, there is no back seat. We climb into a dark cave in the back and sit right down on the floorboard where there's a nasty piece of old carpet he has flattened out for us to sit on. When we get off the pavement onto the dirt and rocks, the tires start to bump. We fly up, hit our heads and fall around on each other until we reach the church. By the time I get out, my dress is rumpled and my hair's a mess.

"Donna, look here," Uncle Ezzie holds up his hat. "You sat on it and crushed it. But that's okay, baby."

I love my uncle Ezzie.

We know all the verses to one hymn, "Come to the Church in the Wild Wood." On the second verse, all I do is sing, "Come, come, come, come," and Alexis has a solo.

*There's a church in the valley by the wildwood,*
*No lovelier spot in the dale;*
*No place is so dear to my childhood,*
*As the little brown church in the vale.*

*Come to the church in the wildwood,*
*Oh, come to the church in the dale,*

# Roughneck Daddy: A Memoir

*No spot is so dear to my childhood,*
*As the little brown church in the vale.*
William S. Pitts 1857

The church people love to hear us sing and pat us on the head when we finish. We can belt this one out so you can hear it clear out on the dirt road, a different dirt road every Sunday night.

At one service, the congregation keeps clapping for us so we have to think of another song. We look at each other and don't know what to do. Then I ask the pianist if she can play "My Country 'Tis of Thee" that Miss Marion Dorman taught us at school. That number doesn't please the crowd as much.

I hope I've missed Mother's Sunday night call, I think as I ride home. I don't want to talk. I'm not going to. I'll say I'm sick.

As I come through the kitchen door, "Has Mother called?"

"Yeah. She wants us to come visit this summer," Marilyn says, "I think the band is going on a trip to Florida. You and Jimmy can go."

"What? How?"

"You and I can go on the bus," Jimmy runs in, "It might be fun."

"You want to go, Bubba?"

"Might as well. Nothing to do here. There're some new cousins up there."

"Was she? Ah ... do you think Mother means it?"

"She didn't sound drunk, Donna. She had thought about it," Jimmy was excited.

"What did Daddy and Granny say?"

"They said you could go if I'd go with you."

"Really?" then I get excited thinking about traveling to a big city and having an adventure.

"I say we stay two weeks," Jimmy says, starting to make plans.

"What if I get homesick and want to come home sooner?" But I think, what's the chance of getting bored in a big city?

"We'll have a round-trip ticket on the Greyhound, Donna. We can come home anytime we want to."

"I'll think about it."

# Roughneck Daddy: A Memoir

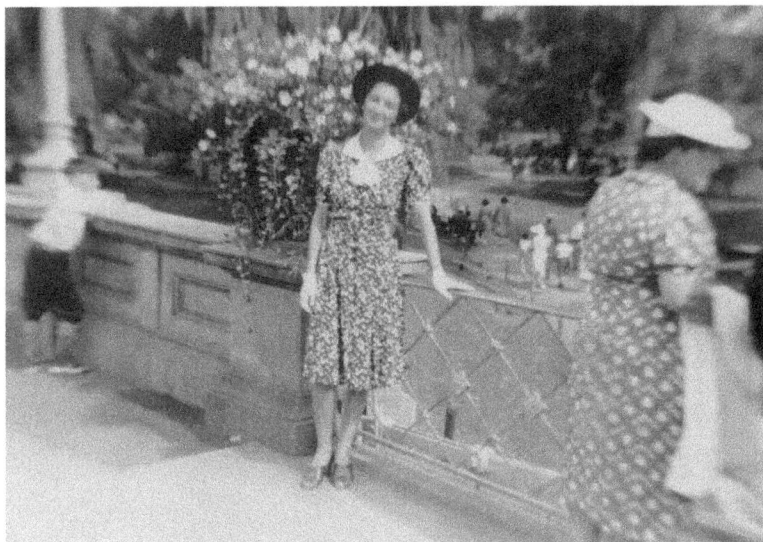

MARION

# - 10 -

# GREYHOUND TO CINCINNATI

After Sunday dinner, I see a stack of greasy dishes
all the way around the kitchen counter. I wash. Marilyn
dries. We do all four verses of "In the Garden" five or six
times, more if it's a Sunday. I take the high part. Makes
the time pass faster. It's me and Marilyn from the glasses
to the black, crusty pots and pans, silverware soaking
under the suds.

*I come to the garden alone,*
*While the dew is still on the roses*
*And the voice I hear, falling on my ear*
*The Son of God discloses*

*And He walks with me, and He talks with me,*
*And He tells me I am His own;*
*And the joy we share as we tarry there,*
*None other has ever known.*

*He speaks, and the sound of His voice,*
*Is so sweet the birds hush their singing,*

## Donna F. Orchard

*And the melody that He gave to me*
*Within my heart is ringing ...*

Marilyn has to dry every blue and white plate and bowl perfectly, so here I stand with drippy dishes.

Daddy and I do everything fast.

At other times, Marilyn uses her Sunday shenanigans. She comes in still in her shirt waist brown plaid dress from church, like she doesn't even see the extra heap of dishes, and chit-chats about going to study with her buddy, Joe. "I'll help you until he comes." But before I'm through with the glasses, honk, honk. "Sorry, Donna. Bye, bye."

Daddy comes in the kitchen, "Don, when you're done, pick out some of those sweet peaches on the back porch to put in the ice cream. I'll get the churn ready."

As we're cranking the ice cream, I have a chance to find out how Daddy feels about our trip to Cincinnati. "Ah, Daddy, do you care if Jimmy and I go to Cincinnati?"

"You've already asked me that, Don. I told you I'd buy the tickets."

"I know, but do you want us to go?" I come out and ask him.

"Sure, I'm glad you're old enough to go to see your mother. I've talked to her about it. I think it's a good idea for you to go up there and spend some time with her. But, Donna, remember this, you can come home on that ticket when you and Jimmy decide you're ready. And you can phone me, sweetie, and talk to Granny and Big Papa too, anytime.

## Roughneck Daddy: A Memoir

"I've never been gone for two weeks, Daddy, and I don't really know Mother. I spent one day with her two years ago when she came to visit."

"You're thirteen years old, Don, and Jimmy will be with you."

"How will we eat and go to the bathroom if we're on the Greyhound for twenty-two hours?" I ask as I pour in more rock salt while Daddy turns the handle and a couple of pieces flip out on the porch as he grinds.

"They have a little bathroom right in the back of the bus, Don. I remember taking a bus home from D.C. must have been, let's see, 1938. First time I ever saw a commode on a Greyhound."

I'm proud I caught these peaches right before they were overripe, when Granny takes the culls to make preserves, I eat my ice cream and swirl my spoon around to try to see every peach I picked out. When I have kids, I'm gonna stay with them. I don't even know my Mother, just that strange voice on the phone, and she laughs a lot when nobody else does.

No matter how hot it gets, there's a breeze on this front porch. I look over at Daddy and think he might stay in that rocking chair a few minutes. I want a big front porch like this one day and a home where everybody shows up on holidays to eat turkey and cornbread dressing. Granny and I start the Thanksgiving meal a week ahead of time, I crumble cornbread; she does sweet potatoes. The pumpkin pies and pound cakes sit in the pie safe, ready.

## Donna F. Orchard

It's fun around here when my aunts and uncles visit. I notice that the Fulmer women mostly get their way. I decide it's because we're as big and tall as the men and just as loud and fight just as hard for what we think's right. My first cousin works for the governor in Baton Rouge. She says she has to "work the crowd," whatever that means. She writes all the governor's speeches and then he talks like he does it. But now, he might go to jail. She drives a real nice car.

The adults sit at the long table, the kids at the card table. The grown-ups tell the old stories again and pretend they're doing it for us. Like the time Daddy came in tired from the rig, picked up a big jar of buttermilk from the icebox and took a slug. "It was Granny's starch!" They all roar and pound Daddy on the back.

That reminds them of the other milk story. We have a half gallon of sweet milk delivered to the porch every day, always in the same place, right in front of the white column. You can't just take a swig. Granny has to pour off the heavy yellow cream that floats on the top to use later for gravy and banana pudding. One day I was in a hurry and turned over about half a jug in the icebox. I didn't clean it up well because Daddy came in later and asked who wasted the milk. "I sure didn't," I spoke up. Then I turned around, stuck my head in the box to get a glass of milk and said, "I hope I don't spill that milk again." I don't know why Daddy thinks that's so funny.

Uncle Lemos from Baton Rouge brings satsumas, a bushel of them, every Christmas. Aunt Sugar and her daughters often take me shopping at Marinsky's, a fancy store on the square. Last year I got an aqua blue wool sweater and a grey plaid skirt. Still fits. I'll pack that in my suitcase to go to Mother's.

It's finally the morning we leave on our trip to Mother's. Daddy swings the door open from the kitchen into the dining room and calls me. He has no idea I haven't slept at all. I don't know what Mother will be like, or a big city like Cincinnati, or anything—it has to be nothing but fun compared to Homer.

Jimmy and I will get on a Greyhound bus thirty miles away in Minden, but not at a real station. Daddy says we have to be on time at four o'clock in the morning by the railroad tracks. In about two days with all the stops, we'll get there.

"Now, sit right behind the driver and don't talk to strangers," Daddy warns.

Granny says, "Tell the driver where you're going and let him know you two are traveling alone. I packed lunches for the first day."

I peek in the bag that's chock-full of meat loaf sandwiches, tea cakes, and even some lemonade in a Mason jar.

When the driver stops, it's still dark. He throws our bags in the luggage compartment below. I thought I would have more time to tell my daddy goodbye. He gives Jimmy and me one of those tight Daddy hugs so I can hardly breath, longer than usual. He rubs the top of my head as always and messes up my hair. I can still see him through the tinted glass, but he can't see me. I watch Daddy drive away until the blue Ford is a little speck.

I look in the face of each smutty, ragtag man watching me from all the rows clear to the back of the bus. Guess they decided they didn't need a shave to ride a Greyhound. Any one of them could be that serial killer on the news. There's a bad smell in here, too. Granny says 'bouquet' for smell. She says it's more ladylike, but I think she'd even agree there's no sweet bouquet on this bus.

One day, I'll get me a ticket on an airplane.

"Hey, Bubba, I wonder what Mother will have for us to eat."

"Probably some of those store-bought cookies she sends for Christmas in the tin, crumbled up by the time they get to us."

"I do like those candies she sends, the chocolate ones with tiny white beads on top. Nothing comes close to Granny's tea cakes though. I think I'll have a tea cake right now."

"Don't eat your lunch already, fat girl."

"Shut up."

I'm a little worried that Mother will be drunk, but not enough to keep me from going. I want to find out why Mother thinks I'm so special. Nobody else seems to think I'm very special, except Daddy because I'm one of his 'three good kids.'

While Jimmy naps, I have the driver's ear for miles, enough time to tell him my whole life story, leaving out the bad parts. "My Uncle Benny is bringing my mother to the bus station to meet us." I don't mention I hardly know my own mother. "Would you like one of my Granny's tea cakes?"

"No, thanks."

"Well I guess that was stupid of me. You can't drive a big bus like this and steer, and watch the road, and control everything, and eat tea cakes."

"Uh huh. Don't you think you need to take a little rest like your brother?"

My lunch is all gone after a few hours and I'm nibbling on Jimmy's.

"Hey, stay out of my sack, Donna."

In the middle of the night, we have a layover in Tennessee; both lunches have been gone miles back. We get off the bus with our own riffraff and go in the dirty, crowded bus station to stand squeezed up against Memphis riffraff. Jimmy hears a man ask me for a cigarette, "Come stand close to me, Donna. Did you see a hamburger joint? I'm hungry. Don't any of these places have a café?"

Not one place to sit and we have an hour. I'm not going through that filthy door to the woman's restroom and get caught in there alone. I'll wait until I'm back on the bus.

No matter how hungry I am, I'm not moving from this spot. I'll make a racket if somebody tries to grab me. Facing the station door, I figure I can kick somebody right out on the street with my big legs if I have to. I'll make them sorry they picked on me.

At once, I look over in a corner and I don't believe my eyes, there's Elvis smiling at me. Well, truth is, I know he's not Elvis, but the closest thing to him in that bus station. He has on a black western suit, snaps on the curvy pockets, and red embroidery at the shoulders; a guitar slung over his back. I'm not gonna smile at any stranger even if he is Elvis. In a minute he walks over, "Are you two alright?" he asks in a gentle voice.

"We're fine," Jimmy assures him.

"Where ya goin'?"

"Cincinnati," Jimmy sounds a little scared.

"How long you been on the bus?"

"About twelve hours," Jimmy cuts him off.

"Have you two had anything to eat?"

"No!"

"Hush, Donna. Yes, sir, our Granny packed us a lunch. But we would like to get a bite if there's a café close by."

"Let's see. I'll be back in a minute."

Elvis is going to save us. I know he is. He's the handsomest man in the world.

When he gets back he says, "There's a bar across the street that serves food. Come on, you have thirty minutes until your bus leaves."

"No, thank you, sir. Don't think my granny would find that place suitable for my sister."

In a minute, he comes back with a policeman. "I've known Jake here for a long time. He's on street patrol every night outside this downtown station. You'll be safe.

I'll buy you something to eat. He'll be right outside the bar."

I look up as we walk across the street and see the red letters "EAT" blink across the black sky.

"I've never sat at a bar before," I try to smooth things over since Jimmy is being short with the man like he's a convict.

"Good. Where you guys from?"

"Louisiana." I order a hamburger, French fries, and a soft drink. "Oh, and a hamburger to go."

"So what takes you two to Cincinnati?"

"We're going to see our mother. If we don't get there tomorrow at noon, she'll call Louisiana, or the police, or who knows what else. We can't miss the bus," I tell him.

"I'll be sure you're on the right one," Elvis says, and in a few minutes he tells the bartender to give him the check.

I can't remember if he said where he was going. I turn around to ask when we board our bus but he's disappeared. I thought I might have imagined the whole thing but later when Jimmy is asleep, I look inside the bag and there's a hamburger.

Soon, all the tough guys tumble back in their seats and go to sleep too. I'm an expert at staying awake to watch the center line. After an hour or so, I notice the bus goes right on top of the white line a few times. Then as the night wears on, the wheels begin to go all the way over into the other lane. The driver whips back with a jerk. He's about to fall asleep! After I ride with my daddy drunk all these years, I'm gonna get killed

on a Greyhound bus with all these crazies. We'll lay out
on here on the road for days while they try to find their
next of kin. God does have a sense of humor.

I punch Jimmy and whisper, "Bubba, wake up, this
driver's about to go to sleep."

"Leave me alone, Donna."

"No, I mean it. We might crash."

"I said, get off me!"


I guess I finally fall asleep, exhausted, because I have
a dream about Mother the night we were snatched. I've
had this same dream before.

Mother comes in early that morning dressed in
her pretty clothes, ready to walk Jimmy and Marilyn to
school. She opens the door. It's too quiet. Something's
not right. I hear the fast clack of her heels across the
floor. When she gets to our beds, she yells, "Jimmy? Marilyn? Baby, where are you?"

She slings open the closet, empty hangers swing
back and forth, she jerks out the drawers, empty. She
sticks her head out of the bathroom window, high
on the third floor, to look into the backyard. No kids
playing outside. All of a sudden, she's running down
the street, but she's in the middle of the road. When
she gets to the school, she wants to see us lined up in
front her, to see her children with her own eyes. "Their
Daddy brought them in. Will you send them out to see
me a minute?"

She waits.

"Marilyn hasn't made it in today, or Jimmy. None of the children are here. I'm sorry."

Mother cries as she walks home alone. She lies in bed and cries all that day and for many days. No calls to my Uncle Benny or calls to Louisiana. Her friends at morning Mass wonder where she is.

Jimmy shakes me, "You're crying, Donna. You must have had a nightmare. Don't cry; it's just a dream."

Suddenly the bus makes a sharp turn and runs up on a grassy place coming down with a bang, all the passengers tossed awake.

"I told you so, Jimmy."

"Shut up. What's going on?"

We finally stop to pick up more people and I see the driver return with a big cup of coffee. I still have my special mental powers.

I memorized which states we go through on the map at home. I didn't put my finger on Indiana. We should go straight through Kentucky and into Cincinnati by noon the second day. When I see the sign, "Welcome to Indiana," I try not to blare out, "Do we go through the state of Indiana on the way to Cincinnati, Ohio?"

Jimmy says, "Leave him alone, Donna. He's the driver." Jimmy's shy like that. He wouldn't ask a question if it meant we stayed in Indiana the rest of our life.

"I have to go around that way to pick some people up for a convention, young lady. We'll only be four or five hours late getting to Cincinnati."

"Only four or five hours late! Mister, we can't be late. You don't understand, my mother will be worried."

"This happens all the time. She'll find out about the change at the station. Now you just sit back and relax, little lady. I'll get you to Cincinnati."

"Sit back, Donna, and let the man drive," Jimmy says, pulling on my arm.

"Jimmy, you know mother will cry and scream when we don't show up. This is the first time we've tried a trip like this. She called twice a day, every day, before we left."

I hope she doesn't have another nervous breakdown. I asked Granny what that was. She said that's when people crack up.

"Benny may not be able to bring Mother back later to pick us up. What if nobody's there?"

"It'll be okay, Donna, eat your hamburger." Jimmy looks over at me, "You could have told them to hold the onion. Gee."

As we finally pull into the station in Cincinnati, I see a woman with red eyes holding her hand at her neck craning to see in every window. I remember now, Marilyn looks like Mother with her thick, dark hair. I see the silk pink and white flowered dress, white beads, and her pretty long legs in high heels as she runs along by the bus. I hope I'll be as beautiful as she is even if I can't be a ballerina.

When we stop, Mother waves for the driver to open up. I see people smiling when she squeals, "My babies, my babies," and won't let us go. "We're going to King's Island, a Reds game, downtown to Pogue's Bargain Basement … Let me look at you," Mother insists, "I was so worried. I called Jim in Louisiana and he said he put you on the bus. Where did they take you kids? You were supposed to be here at eight o'clock last night. It's four in the morning. They kept telling me your bus was delayed and told me to go on home, but I wasn't about to leave without you."

"I think we were lost," Jimmy tries to explain; "I wasn't sure where we were."

"We were in Indiana," I speak up. 'Welcome to Indiana.' I knew we weren't supposed to be in that state. When the driver told us at eight o'clock we're due into Cincinnati in five or six more hours, I hung onto the back of his seat; told him he can expect a police car to be right beside us any minute, chasing him down. If I were you, I'd watch for the blue lights. He didn't understand you'd be looking for us. I told him you'd track us down with the CIA, the FBI and the National Guard, you'll see. The only thing he said was, 'Aw right kid. Sit back and relax.'"

"We're glad you're here, guys," a man says as he walks up with our bags.

"Jimmy, you remember my brother, Benny, don't you? Donna, you were too young to remember when we lived in Cincinnati."

"Sure, hi." I don't think Jimmy is telling the truth.

"You had us worried about you." I know that Benny is my uncle, but Mother doesn't introduce him as Uncle Benny, just Benny. He's warm and friendly, but red faced like Mother. "I know you two are starved. We'll stop for cheese conies. You'll love 'em. Skyline Chili. Open all

night. Cincy's known for our chili dogs, coleslaw, sauer-
kraut, the works. You have to eat two or three; they're
little. We'll get a big bag full, and take 'em to Kinsey,
Marion."

"Those kids couldn't wait until you got here. Ted
just turned thirteen years old, Donald is eleven, Barry
is nine, and Geri is four, the only little girl," Benny says
and seems very happy and proud of all his kids.

"They've been up and down my stairs for a week
asking about you," Mother cackles and I notice some
missing teeth. "They've got something planned for every
minute you're here."

"Yeah, how ya like living down there in the South?"
Benny asks as he pulls into Skyline.

I don't want to answer. It's the only place I've ever
lived.

"The kids will show you Cincinnati," He looks
around as he throws the tall sack of hot dogs in the car.
I smell the buns and imagine them overflowing with
cheese and chili. I wish I could grab one right now.

"It's half price night at King's Island on Saturday.
If you have time to rest up, we'll go out there tonight,"
Benny says, sounding as excited as we are.

"Keep those kids at home this morning so Donna
and Jimmy can get some sleep, Benny," Mother insists.

"We're alright," Jimmy said as we nod. "I don't even
feel tired," then whispers to me, "This is going to be fun."

I pull my suitcase up the narrow stairs to Mother's
third floor flat on Kinsey Avenue. She goes on and on
about Cincinnati built on seven hills. She was born on

## Roughneck Daddy: A Memoir

Price Hill, and has lived here most of her life. I'm out of breath, but Mother bounces up easily.

Mother is happy when these stairs are full of activity the next week, loud talking, loud laughing, kids either coming or going. "Got a sandwich, Marion?" one of the kids is bound to ask. She hates the quiet and mundane. She loves a good story.

Mother looks down the hall, "Is Lillibun's coming up the steps behind you?" Mother asks my cousin Ted, the oldest of Buddy's kids. "He's usually with you when he knows there's lunch," she roars.

"His name is Lillicrap, Marion; and I haven't seen him today." Ted looks at Jimmy, "Marion calls him Lillibuns behind his back; says she can't say his name. She's a trip."

When the boys go out for the day, Mother puts a Dean Martin single on the Victrola, and we dance around the room.

*Sweet, sweet memories you gave-a me*
*You can't beat the memories you gave-a me'*

*Take one fresh and tender kiss*
*Add one stolen night of bliss*
*One girl, one boy*
*Some grief, some joy*
*Memories are made of this*

"Dino. He's a handsome dog," Mother swoons.

"Mother, I don't like being taller than all the boys in my class. I've never been on a date. I think that's why. I mostly dance with girls at the Co-Cola plant, our teen club. I feel embarrassed to dance with a boy with his head buried in my chest."

"You're only thirteen years old, honey. One day you'll be glad you're tall."

When Mother goes to the grocery store, I poke around and find her old yellow scrapbook album that she brought to Louisiana one time. I have a bow in my hair in one of my baby pictures, and in another shot, I 'm wearing a little gold bracelet. Jewelry is an extra at Big Papa's house, like orange juice—no one buys it.

I want to find out about Marion Denton, the dancer. She saved letters from producers, contracts for shows, playbills, even menus from fancy hotels.

I read some of Mother's birthday cards, even one from me, and remember—Mother was born on Valentine's Day. That's why she has all of her will-o-'the-wisp romantic notions; why she keeps old faded love poems she cries over every time she picks one up and keeps pictures of old boyfriends before she met Daddy. She can find a card that makes me cry—on Halloween. And Dino. She sings along with Dean Martin, swirling around the room and pretending, she's really dancing with him. I love that about my mother.

*SAMUELS ATTRACTIONS, INC.*
*Suite 1312—1560 Broadway*
*Sept. 6*th *1932*

*To Mr. Adolphus % Roxy Theatre*
*West 50*th *St. N.Y.*

*This will introduce*

*Miss Marion Denton*
*Ballet*

*Marion Denton of Dorothy Byton's Revue seen at Albee*
*Please call Friday April 21 from 12 to 1 o'clock with rehearsal*
*clothes*

*Joe Price Dance Studio*
*Eaves Bldg. 151 West 46*th *Street*

*Geo. P. Gross*

## Donna F. Orchard

*September 19, 1932*
*Cincinnati, Ohio*

*Miss Marion Denton*
*332 W. 51st Street*
*New York City*

*Dear Marion,*

*How are you getting along in the big city with its bright lights? It must have made you feel good to get back on old Manhattan (sic) Island again, to review the old land marks and show houses that was familiar to you when you were on the RKO circuit. Mr. Hutchison told me that you are with a show called "Amateur (sic) Night in London …*

I hear Mother coming up the stairs.

"Can you help me, honey? Grab these bags on the landing."

"Sure."

"Sorry it took me so long, Don. I had twenty-five dollars and when she rang me up, the total was thirty-seven dollars and few cents. Anyway, I had to sort through the buggy and see what I needed for dinner tonight and ask her to stick the rest back. I got some of your favorite snacks and saved enough money to walk down to Clifton bakery in the morning, to get a cherry pie for breakfast. It's my favorite; made fresh every day."

"A cherry pie for breakfast sounds wicked, Mother."

## Roughneck Daddy: A Memoir

She never has enough money for all the good things she sees in the grocery store and throws in her buggy. I don't know what she's thinking. It doesn't seem to bother her, while I stand there dying of embarrassment. That's why I didn't go today.

"Mother, I found that old scrapbook of yours. You save everything. I should start saving stuff, but I'm not sure if I have anything important. You were like a movie star."

"You have cards I send you, Don. We'll get a scrapbook for you while you're here."

"Come sit down by me, Mother," I'm anxious. "Now when did you leave home for New York?"

"It was 1926; I was only fourteen years old. Of course, Don, we didn't know the stock market was going to crash in 1929, but surprisingly, the entertainment industry people did better than most during the hard times. The crowds still wanted to go see Fred Astaire and Ginger Rogers and just leave their troubles behind."

"Here's your contract for *Rio Rita*. You only made $35 dollars a week?"

"That was pretty good money at that time, baby."

"Why did you stop dancing, Mother?"

"My feet were the main reason I couldn't dance anymore. See these bunions?" She takes off her shoe. "They hurt me all the time."

"I have bunions already. Look at my foot." I take off my shoe and show her.

"Oh, honey. Take care of your feet. They have to last you a long time … The other reason I left the business was that I was going all over the country in live reviews. Then suddenly theater companies were anticipating the boom in talkies, sound in movies.

When I went to New York, I was working for the big Keith – Albee - Orpheum, the KAO circuit of theaters, built around the time that live vaudeville was fading. Everybody was trying to get into the movie business. It was a crazy time. Joseph Kennedy bought out the company I was working for and the combined company was RKO. After sound movies started, the Ziegfeld's Follies and the live reviews became a thing of the past."

"What did you do then? You weren't married to Daddy were you?" I continue to quiz her.

"Oh, no," She gets up to get another beer. "I hadn't met your daddy yet. After I quit dancing, I went to Boston to work doing demonstrations for a cosmetics company that sold Hollywood Curlers, a new product line that had come out. It was constant traveling. I was lonely."

Mother gets another beer and lies down on the couch.

"My friend Flo, who eventually became my sister-in-law, was in D.C., so I transferred there with the Goodman Company, the hair curler company, and was still doing demonstrations. I loved the German food at the Heidelberg Hotel; knew everybody there. Jim came in as a cook at the hotel."

"Do you remember the first time he kissed you?" She went on like she didn't hear me.

Oh, Don, Jim was a handsome man. Still is. And he was a great dancer."

"Here's the marriage certificate."

*'I hereby certify that on this 18th day of October 1939, at Municipal Court, D.C., James Taylor Fulmer and Marion Denterclausen were by me united in marriage …*

"I figured up that you were twenty-seven years old and he was twenty-nine years old in 1939 when you got married." I continue examining each page.

Mother drinks lots of beer in the evening, gets loud, and then falls asleep. Daddy claims she drinks so much because she's German. She drinks beer at meals instead of water. Her place is very different from my teetotaling Baptist grandparent's home, more exciting and fun, but a little scary.

Tonight is different. Her personality changes from excited to agitated without warning and she starts talking about the Fulmers out of nowhere, then cursing the Fulmers, those sonsofabitches. I try not to let her know I'm quietly sobbing. The Fulmers are the only family I know.

She begins to hold me tight around the waist, maybe because I won't agree with her. I wish Jimmy was here.

She holds me tighter and tighter and finally I yell, "Let me go Mother. It wasn't my fault. You're hurting me."

"You're just like them now, those Southern sonofabitches. Go ahead. Take up for them."

Crying harder I tell her I'm leaving tomorrow. "I'm calling Daddy to pick me up early in Minden." I wish I was home, safe at Granny's, but I really don't want to call. They'd never let me come back to see my mother, ever. I don't know what to do.

As mother's loosens her grip, I look over and see that she's passed out.

When she wakes up the next morning, "Hi, baby. I love you so much. I'm so glad you're here. Let me rub your back. We've got tickets to the Reds game today. We're playing the Chicago Cubs at Crosley."

I've learned the lesson well: Don't mention 'drunk' when the sun comes up the next day.

I stay.

It's the sixth inning at Crosley and the Cubs and Reds are tied. The Reds get a hard hit out to the center field fence. Mother stands up, "Yea, Yea! That's my Reds. A home run. We're ahead!" I wonder why no one around us is standing, when Benny pulls on Mother's skirt, "Why don't ya si'down, Marion." It was an easy catch in center field.

The organ pounds, "Okay, fans, it's Harry Caray and it's the seventh inning stretch at Crosley." Then a boom-ing roar from the crowd, as Chicago and Cincinnati fans stand together, arms in the air, singing and weaving side to side…

## Roughneck Daddy: A Memoir

*Take me out to the ballgame,*
*Take me out with the crowd.*
*Buy me some peanuts and cracker jacks,*
*I don't care if I never get back,*
*Let me root, root, root for the home team,*
*If they don't win it's a shame.*
*For its one, two, three strikes you're out,*
*At the old ballgame.*

## - 11 -

# THE HITCHHIKER

Daddy comes in and carries the big tin canteen to the back porch. It's still frosty so I get a sip, water so icy it hurts my teeth.

Oh, my teeth. "Daddy can you go to the dentist with me today? See this swollen place in the back? I had a toothache all day yesterday."

"Did you put an aspirin on it?"

"I tried that last week. It's bleeding now."

"Have you called Claude? Yeah, said he could take me at 11:00."

"I don't want to go by myself. Please Daddy."

"Baby you know I've got to get some sleep. I feel like a beat dog. I have to leave back out for Beaumont at five. A wildcat close by brought in a gusher last night so Slumber J wants us to work double shifts. Every able-bodied man they can find is out on this job."

Maybe Granny or Big Papa can go with me. No, they'll tell me not to act like a big baby.

I bet I've been lying back in this chair fifteen minutes. I wonder where Dr. Tillman is. I can hear him in the other room grinding and gouging, and grinding again. I asked Daddy if he thought the doctor would drill on me. "I doubt it, Honey." Yeah, he just said that to calm me down. He'll use that jackhammer thing I hear next door. "Ah h h h" comes from the other room for a long time. Seems like a person should be able to come up for air.

I didn't tell Sharon I had an appointment to see her Daddy in case I do something like scream or cry. I'll be at her birthday party Friday. I wonder if they're gonna ship her off to summer camp again after school's out.

I grip the cold arms of the heavy chair tighter and look up at all the steel, sharp dentist things dangling around my head. I'm freezing.

Now my tooth doesn't hurt at all. I probably don't even need to be here.

"Hello, Donna."

"Hi Dr. Tillman."

"What have you and Sharon been up to lately?"

"Just swimming and shooting hoops."

"Well, what can I do for you?"

"My jaw's swollen. See my gum in the back? It hurts sometime, but it's not hurting now. Daddy says I need to put an aspirin in it."

He stretches my mouth open as wide as he can get it and looks in the back. I hate it when people stare at me. "I see. Have you had a fever, Donna? Let me feel your head."

"Jane, will you step in here, please?" he calls for his assistant. She looks in my mouth and rolls her eyes way up where the things are hanging, then lets out one of those disgusted sounds. They go over in the corner to whisper about me. I can't hear what they're saying.

"Well, Donna, this tooth may be too far gone. May have to come out. But I need to get that swelling down. I'll be right back."

By this time I feel the sweat run down my legs. I jump up before I know I'm gonna do it and take a quick look down the hall. The coast is clear to the back door. Next thing I know I'm running through Miss Kinebrew's yard almost home. Then one of the colored's dogs comes after me. Papa says they don't like white people. I make it to the porch.

Oh, God, please don't let Sharon find out.

Granny asks, "How was the dentist, Donna?"

"Just fine."

"Well, what did he do, Baby?"

"Not much. Says the swelling has to go down."

Later Mr. Blanton calls to say he's got some vegetables for us if we'll come get them. "Marilyn you haven't taken me for a ride since you got your license," Granny says.

"Daddy says she can't drive worth a flip. Says he's glad she got her license so he doesn't have to get in the car with her again."

"Well I got my license, didn't I?

"Did you show them the two dents in the Chevy?

"Nobody asked you to go, you little twerp."

"Oh, I'll go so I can call the ambulance."

"Very funny."

"Sure, Granny. I'll take you. See if Jimmy wants to go."

"I call shotgun. Get out of here and let Granny sit up front, Donna."

"Okay, I'll sit in the back and play slap jack with Jimmy."

"Marilyn, I want to go up the hill by Ezzie's and see how Aunt Blondell is. It won't take but a minute," Granny says.

I wish the coloreds over there would put up those dogs. Here they come barking at me. I almost got bit yesterday. And why don't they paint those old broken down houses?"

Marilyn says, "My teacher told us there's no place for coloreds to work in Del City."

"What?"

When we get out on Johnson's Road I notice a man with his thumb up, "Don't slow down, Marilyn. I'm afraid of hitchhikers."

"What do you know about hitchhikers, Donna?" Granny asks.

"Oh, nothing, but you're not supposed to pick up strangers, are you?"

"Oh, Daddy's already told me that." Marilyn says.

Back at home Marilyn calls to me, "Donna, come here and I'll show you how to pluck your eyebrows."

"Just a minute." I go find Jimmy. "Jimmy go down to the patch with me. Marilyn's gonna try to hold me down and torture me again."

"Okay. Let's go."

The next day, since Jimmy doesn't go to church either, he and Daddy go to Lake Bistineau to put out a trot line. He'll go back in a week to check it. Last year he went back and found a 62 lb. buffalo fish on one of his lines. Daddy thought it would be selfish to keep it all for us so he invited the whole town to come to the park one Saturday to eat fried fish.

I might as well not ask Granny if I can go with them. She'll tell me to go on to Sunday School.

"I know I can't go, can I, Daddy?"

"We're just gonna run over there to put that trot line out and come right back, Don. Go on to Sunday School."

"I knew you'd say that."

That night I look at my movie magazine in the living room by the picture window so I'll see Daddy pull up. I'm not gonna close my eyes until they're back. At midnight I decide maybe they're going to stay at the lake all night without me. They've already had a nice supper somewhere. I hate Sunday School.

It gets later and later and I get scared. They could have had a wreck. Daddy shouldn't drink when Jimmy's in the car. I can't figure out where they might be, maybe at the old Ruth's.

About that time I see bright lights in the window. After Daddy pulls up he jumps out and heads down the worn path to his side door. I don't see Jimmy. He must have fallen asleep in the back seat.

I slip out the front and open the car door. Jimmy is down on the seat in the dark. I hear him sniffing. He's crying! I've never seen my Bubba cry even when I kick him as hard as I can in the shins.

"What's wrong, Bubba? Are you crying? Did Daddy get drunk?"

"No. He picked up a hitchhiker. Guy smelled horrible."

"What?"

"He kept driving around and wouldn't let the man out. I saw blood and…"

"Stop! Oh, my gosh! I can hardly hear you. Did you say blood?"

"Got it in his head the man robbed him." I see big tears now and Jimmy doubles up bawling, "Pulled his pocket knife out on him."

"Stop! I'm going to hold my ears."

"The guy yelled, ' Jesus, Jesus, please don't kill me!'"

"I don't believe you. Stop. I won't listen. Not my daddy!"

Jimmy sobs and chokes, "Held the knife to his neck while the man begged, while he begged Daddy not to cut him."

"I'm not listening. It's not true. Daddy wouldn't do that to anybody. My daddy's not mean. He just got drunk."

## Roughneck Daddy: A Memoir

"He was sober, I swear. I yelled at him over and over to let the guy out. He finally slowed down and threw the man out in an alley in Shreveport. Found his billfold on the car seat when we stopped. It was two hours, and…"

"I'm gonna to be sick."

I turn and run in the pitch-black down by Mamie's and around by Hazel Kup's. I bend over when I feel pain gush up in my throat. I can't see anything, but I must be at Uncle Ezzie's when I hear that dog get after me again. I run and run and try to outrun him. All of a sudden I'm on the ground. I just sit there. Everything's black and the dog's not barking. I hold my sides to vomit, but all that comes out is groan like an animal in a deep well, a sound I've never made before.

Where am I? I smell motor oil and feel my greasy hands. That's what I slipped on. Seems like this alley is one of my short cuts.

I look around the corner and can make out railroad cars. I didn't know I was this far from home. Then I bump up against a pole, look up, and see the letters Western Auto. Oh, I'm near the house we rented when we lived with Ruth Switch-a-roo and her boys.

I know how to get home now. Only thing is I have to walk by that haunted house where there's no lights.

Daddy uses that same knife to peel sugar cane for me to suck on. He never touches me when he gets mad. How could he do this?

Why did he pick the man up anyway? He's never done that when I was in the car.

He must have gone crazy. Could he hurt me?

No, I bet if I had been in the car this never would have happened. He made Jimmy a prisoner just like the hitchhiker. How can he go and scare Jimmy to death? When I see his face I'm going to jump on him and pound him with my fists and kick him as hard as I can.

I have heard the stories that Big Papa hit Daddy when he was a little boy. I know he drinks too much. But, this time he can't just mumble his same old prayer "I'm a "dirty, rotten sinner."

None of his brothers act like this. They're kind men. When mother neglected us, somehow I knew she was sick. She was in the hospital three times.

Was he really sober like Jimmy said?

Could my daddy just be mean?

# REFERENCES

McKinney, B.B. editor (1940) "In the Garden" *Broadman Hymnal* (Nashville: The Broadman Press).

Mitchell, Joni (1971) "Carey" Reprise.
Pitts, Dr. William S. (1857) "Oh, Come to the Church in the Wildwood." *Great Songs of the Church No.2.* http: // www.vaughns-1-pagers.com/music/church-hymns htm

Weldon, Frank/Cavanaugh, James (1936) "I Like Mountain Music" http:www lyrics playground.com/alpha/ songs.shtml